Wisbech
1800~1901

Andrew C Ingram

Andrew C. Ingram

MP Middleton Press

Cover picture: The northern side of Wisbech Market Place, photographed on a busy Saturday in 1895 by John Kennerell. A market had been held here since at least 1200. Wares on sale include baskets, trunks, bowls, jugs, fabrics and fishing pots. This view features a dozen commercial premises, of which five - the Golden Lion, George, Mermaid, Ship and Griffin - are public houses. (A.Ingram collection)

Published November 2002

ISBN 1 901706 93 1

© Middleton Press, 2002

Design Deborah Esher

Published by
   Middleton Press
   Easebourne Lane
   Midhurst, West Sussex
   GU29 9AZ
Tel: 01730 813169
Fax: 01730 812601

Printed & bound by Biddles Ltd,
   Guildford and Kings Lynn

CONTENTS

ACKNOWLEDGEMENTS

I am most grateful to the following for their assistance in the preparation of this book: M.Allen, C.Bedford, R.Bell, V.Bolam, P.Clayton, G.Dunlop, R.Fairhead, R.Green, Dr S.Greer, P.Harvey, H.Lilley, A.Oakford, G.Smith, C.Swaine, Rev W.Zwalf, the staff at Cambridge University Library, Lambeth Palace Library, Wisbech Library, Wisbech & Fenland Museum, Wisbech Town Council. Extracts from Queen Victoria's Journal are published with the permission of Her Majesty Queen Elizabeth II. A special word of thanks to my wife Jenny, for her support and encouragement.

GEOGRAPHICAL SETTING

The Cambridgeshire market town of Wisbech has been described as one of the most attractive towns of East Anglia. Flowing through this historic Capital of The Fens is the River Nene, flanked by one of the finest Georgian brick streets of England.

In Norman times Wisbech had been situated at the confluence of the River Nene and Welle Stream, just three miles from the sea. A castle guarded the town's Market Place and wooden river bridge, whilst a ferry crossed the broad Welle Stream estuary. Four hundred years of fen drainage and land reclamation has now left Wisbech situated ten miles inland but with some of the best growing land in Britain. This combination of fertile soil, busy markets and navigable waterways created a prosperity that is still reflected in the town's rich architectural heritage.

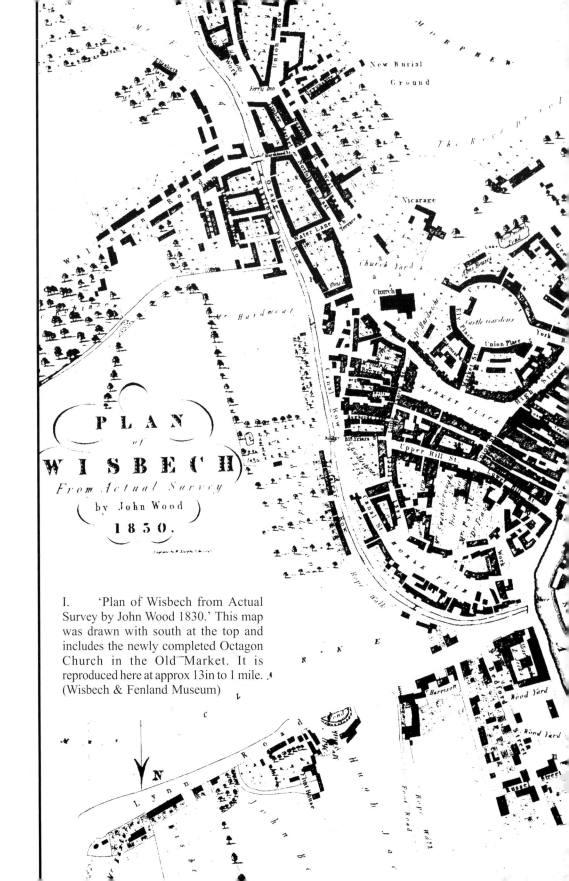

PLAN
of
WISBECH
From Actual Survey
by John Wood
1830.

I. 'Plan of Wisbech from Actual Survey by John Wood 1830.' This map was drawn with south at the top and includes the newly completed Octagon Church in the Old Market. It is reproduced here at approx 13in to 1 mile. (Wisbech & Fenland Museum)

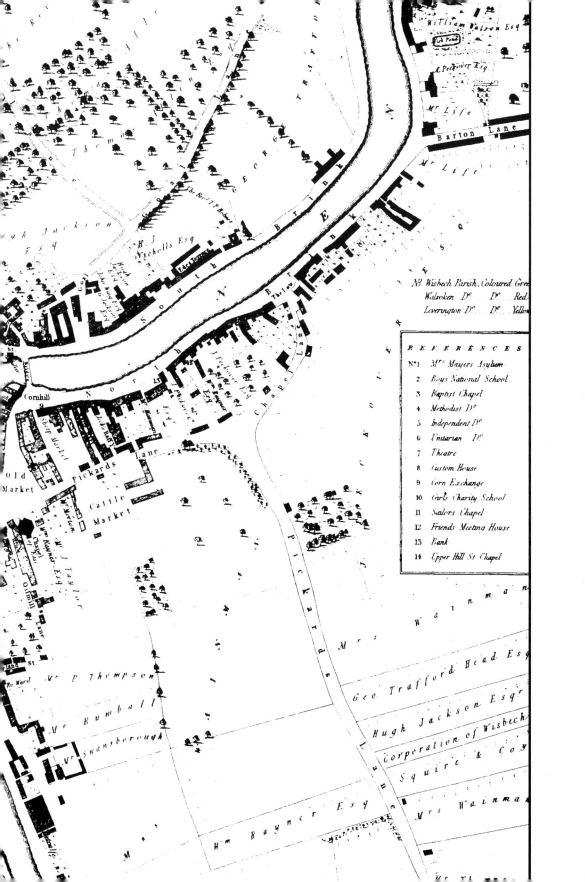

REFERENCES

Nº 1 Mrs Mayers Asylum
2 Boys National School
3 Baptist Chapel
4 Methodist Dº
5 Independent Dº
6 Unitarian Dº
7 Theatre
8 Custom House
9 Corn Exchange
10 Girls Charity School
11 Sailors Chapel
12 Friends Meeting House
13 Bank
14 Upper Hill St Chapel

NB. Wisbech Parish, Coloured Green
Walsoken Dº   Dº   Red
Leverington Dº   Dº   Yellow

HISTORICAL BACKGROUND

In 1800 a Corporation, consisting of ten elected members led by a Town Bailiff administered the town of Wisbech. In 1610 James I renewed their Charter of Incorporation, granted by Edward VI in 1549, when the elected men became known as Capital Burgesses. Under the provisions of the 1835 Municipal Corporations Act, Wisbech established a governing body composed of a Mayor, Aldermen and Councillors. Henry Leach, the last Town Bailiff, became Mayor of the newly formed Borough of Wisbech. They held their meetings in the upper storey of Exchange Hall, the Council Chamber being rebuilt in 1872 to create a more lofty and spacious hall.

The origins and spelling of the name 'Wisbech' has caused confusion for both residents and visitors. The Saxon spelling was 'Visebec' whilst the Doomsday Book had 'Wisebece' and the 1379 Holy Trinity Seal 'Wysbech'. The Universal British Directory of 1794 stated that *the original name was Ouzebeach, the beach or outfall of the River Ouse, which flowed into the Welle Stream.* In his 1898 history F.J.Gardiner writes that *the original town [Wysebec] is believed to have been built between the two rivers, the Wyse, a little stream or 'bec' from Guyhirn, and the Great Ouse, the large river from Littleport.* Pigot's Directory of 1830 notes that both 'Wisbeach' and 'Wisbech' were in common use. The Corporation finally resolved to drop the 'a' in response to requests by postal and railway companies for a uniform spelling.

Queen Victoria described Wisbech as *A very curious town. The canal runs through the middle of the streets and the masts of ships intermingled with the houses gives a very curious effect to the place.* The Wisbech Canal had opened in 1796 along the course of the Welle Stream to permit navigation between Wisbech and the Old Nene at Outwell. The Port of Wisbech had received large vessels since the 13th century but by 1800 only barges and small ships could navigate through the silting course of the river. The canal, which took its waters from the Nene, was also plagued by silt settling out and blocking the sluice gates.

The Nene Outfall Works of the 1820s, which had cost Wisbech some £45,000, lowered the riverbed, whilst the Woodhouse Marsh Cut of 1830 straightened a portion of the river. Tonnage duties received by the Corporation reflected the improved draught for vessels, from 29,242 tons in 1805 and 70,320 in 1825; it had increased again to 159,678 tons by 1845. In 1852 the Nene Valley Commissioners planned to improve the river from Wisbech into Northamptonshire. The river began silting up again when contractors built dams across the river at Waldersea and Guyhirn 'for the temporary purpose of excavating the river'. When the Commissioners ignored demands by Wisbech Corporation to remove the dams its citizens took matters into their own hands and destroyed them.

The opening of the Wisbech to March railway in 1847 combined with the river improvements created a period of sustained growth. In 1841 the town's population stood at 8530, but by 1851 this had increased by 19% to 10,178. The railway also created the need for standardised time and in 1852 Greenwich Mean Time, also known as Railway Time, was introduced throughout Britain. Many local people had taken their first train journey in 1851 to view The Great Exhibition, held in the Crystal Palace. Organised by Prince Albert it was an unqualified success and marked a transformation in the middle Victorian period.

On 3rd February 1897 the *Wisbech Advertiser* reported that *pedestrians along the Lynn Road were somewhat startled on Sunday evening at the appearance of a snorting horseless vehicle careering towards the town. It turned out to be one of the new motor cars, the very first to enter the town. The three occupants of this Arnold Victoria ultimately found a resting-place at the Rose and Crown Hotel. About ten o'clock the engine was started, and the motor car made several circuits of the Market Place. Afterwards the car, which travels along fair road easily at a rate of 10 miles per hour, proceeded at a rapid pace along High Street.* The twentieth century was just around the corner.

THE OCTAGON CHURCH

In 1801 the population of Wisbech stood at 4710. By 1821 this figure had grown to 6515 representing an increase of 38%, compared to the average for England and Wales of 34%. In the same period church congregations throughout England and Wales had increased dramatically. Church of England communicants increased by 6.5% to 570,000, whilst in just twenty years the Methodist movement had grown from 91,825 to 215,466 - an increase of 134%.

Between 1802 and 1881 a total of seventeen churches and chapels were built in Wisbech, most replacing earlier structures or rented rooms. At a meeting in the Sessions House on 24th June 1825 Dr Abraham Jobson, vicar of St Peter's parish church, offered £2000 in stock and the purchase of ten £50 shares towards the building of a Chapel of Ease. This 'overflow' church had no separate parish but would ease the pressure on St Peter's where packed congregations would listen to sermons lasting an hour.

On 24th November 1825 'A Meeting of the Inhabitants of Wisbech relative to the Erection of the proposed Chapel of Ease' heard that Dr Jobson had increased his offer to a £4000 donation and the purchase of twenty subscription shares at £50 each. The total cost of the building was estimated at £10,000. The letting of 'sittings' at £50 each soon raised £6000, whilst Dr Jobson's generous donation covered the balance. He also endowed the Chapel with an estate covering 263 acres for the benefit of the incumbent. Joseph Taylor had previously made two offers for the sale of part of his estate opposite the Cattle Market as a site for the intended chapel, but the meeting resolved to erect it on a site in the Old Market. The first Chapel Wardens, Robert Hardwicke and James Brecknock Palmer, were both subscribers.

Although sufficient funds were available for constructing the chapel, a grant application was made to the Church Building Society for vaults. At that time body snatching was prevalent with corpses being dug up in churchyards and then sold to medical students for dissection. The total cost of these vaults was around £3000, offset by a grant of £1200. The Wisbech Chapel of Ease Octagon Ledger for 1832 lists seventeen vault purchases. Rev F.Holmes purchased vault no.11 for £16 4s 0d on 10th May 1831, whilst Mrs Francis Edwards paid just £1 5s 0d on 13th September 1843 for a vault 10ft under the Chancel. A doorway under the right-hand staircase of the Octagon's south porch led down into the crypt.

In their *History of Wisbech and The Fens* published in 1849 Walker & Craddock described the church interior. *Its construction, though tending to draw the congregation round the speaker, is so mismanaged, that in some parts of the chapel, where the hearers are nearest the pulpit, it is with difficulty the words of the preacher can be distinguished. Two or three perceptible voices, glancing from different faces of the chapel, cross one another, and render either reading or preaching in such parts indistinct. The gallery looms over the floor of the chapel, making its paltry proportions appear less. The architect, in consequence of his unfortunate design, was obliged to place the pulpit in front of the chancel arch, thereby hiding all that part of the chapel from view; and sundry long cracks in this part give threatenings, before the edifice is twenty years old, of instability.*

On Thursday 13th January 1831 the Wisbech Chapel of Ease was consecrated by the Bishop of Lincoln, acting for the Bishop of Ely. Two weeks later Henry Fardell, a son-in-law of the Bishop of Ely, was inducted as Dr Jobson's replacement at St Peter's. Rev Fardell kept a diary during his ministry, which contained a number of references to the Octagon. His entry for 19th April 1835, Easter Sunday, notes *The Clerk stated that many families attended the sacrament at the Chapel [of Ease], who were accustomed to receive it at St Peter's, in consequence of the great number of communicants.* His entry for 15th May 1842 - Whit Sunday noted: *A bad practice prevails of numbers leaving St Peter's for the purpose of attending the Sacrament at the Chapel of Ease, as was today with the following . . . on the ground that they are not so long detained.*

1: 1800-1809

1.   Wisbech parish church is seen in an engraving published on 1st October 1800 for the Revd Caesar Morgan, Vicar of Wisbech. This fine Norman building dates from 1187 with later additions and rebuilding in a variety of architectural styles. In a room above the Decorated-style south porch members of the Guild of the Holy Trinity were educating boys by 1379. The Guild's chapel, built circa 1500 in the Perpendicular style, is on the right.
(Wisbech & Fenland Museum)

22mm William III farthing

17mm Anne 3d

2.   To accommodate a growing congregation wooden galleries were erected in St Peter's between the mid-17th and early 19th century, increasing seating capacity to 1600. These galleries not only placed an increased strain on the church fabric, but also drastically reduced the amount of light entering the building. (Wisbech & Fenland Museum)

3.   A selection of machine-produced 'milled' coins, from the reigns of William III to George III, that would have appeared in the church's offertory plate around 1800. The clergy had requested a tithe, one tenth of an income, to support their ministry and then in April 1799 the government introduced a 10% income tax. The great recoinage of 1696 had removed from circulation the earlier clipped and badly worn hand-made 'hammered' coins. This had been financed by imposing a 'Window Tax', finally repealed in 1851. Actual sizes of coins shown in millimetres. (C.Cooke)

26mm George I 1/- *33mm George II 2/6d* *21mm George III 6d*

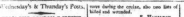

4.   *The Lynn and Wisbech Packet*, the first newspaper to be circulated in Wisbech, contained little local news. Published by Turner and Whittingham of King's Lynn with Mr White of Wisbech acting as their agent, the first edition appeared on Tuesday 7th January 1800. The government had imposed a duty of 3d per pound weight on newsprint; the sixpence cover price also included three-halfpence stamp duty. A duty of 3s 6d per advertisement, however brief, also had to be paid before publication. (Wisbech & Fenland Museum)

II.   In the parish of Wisbech St Peter the church was dedicated to Saint Peter and Saint Paul. The Arms of the Town of Wisbech depict the crossed keys of St Peter, for in St Matthew's gospel Jesus said to Peter *I will give unto thee the keys of the kingdom of heaven.* These Alms were featured on a 13th century boss above the north aisle and on the 16th century tower of St Peter's Church. The Corn Hall, Butter Cross and Working Men's Institute pediments also featured this design. (A.Ingram collection)

5.   Introduced in the reign of Charles II guineas were minted from gold imported by the Africa Company from Guinea. With a face value of 21 shillings this George III 'spade' guinea, minted between 1787 and 1799, inspired brass imitations for use as counters in card games. Last minted in 1813 the guinea coin was replaced in 1817 by the sovereign, although the guinea was still a unit of reckoning especially in horse racing. (C.Cooke)

25mm

Isle of Ely.

AT the GENERAL QUARTER SESSIONS *of the Peace, holden at Wisbech St. Peter's, in and for the Isle of Ely, on Wednesday the fifteenth Day of January, One thousand Eight hundred :—*

IT WAS ORDERED that no Person or Persons making Bread for Sale within the said Isle of Ely, should, *after the Sixteenth Day of February* next, make or expose to Sale any other Sort or Sorts of Bread, purporting to be of a superior Quality, or sold at a higher Price than the STANDARD WHEATEN BREAD. And that the said Order should continue in force for the space of three Calendar Months, from the said Sixteenth Day of February, unlefs sooner revoked at some General or Adjourned Quarter Sessions of the Peace for the said Isle of Ely, and that the same should be published in the Cambridge Newspaper and Copies thereof be stuck up in the principal Towns and Villages within the said Ifle of Ely.

JAMES BELLAMY,

Dep. Clerk, of the Peace, for the Ifle of Ely.

6.   Rev Abraham Jobson was appointed vicar of St Peter's in 1802, with a stipend of £700 per annum. He discovered that owners of grasslands in the parish had claimed exemption from the church's demand for a tithe. After five years of legal wrangling Dr Jobson won his case in the Higher Courts, increasing his annual income to around £2000. He was generous with his new-found wealth, providing books to encourage singing in St Peter's Church and helping to establish Sunday Schools in neighbouring villages. He also served as Wisbech Town Bailiff in 1811 and contributed towards a Girls' School in Lower Hill Street.
(G.Garford/Wisbech Town Council)

12mm

36mm

34mm

7.   These George III pennies illustrate the great monetary changes that took place during his sixty-year reign (top). Escalating silver prices caused by the Napoleonic Wars resulted in few silver coins being minted. Until the early 19th century coins usually contained metal equivalent to their face value. In 1797 Matthew Boulton's steam-powered coining press produced the first copper 'cartwheel' penny [centre] to replace the silver penny. Prior to 1800 only half-pennies and farthings had been minted in copper. A George III penny of reduced weight (lower) was minted in 1806 to replace the bulky 1oz cartwheel.
(C.Cooke)

8.   The Shambles, a two-storey wooden building, was erected at the eastern end of the Market Place in 1588. The upper floor was used for the storage of corn or flour, whilst butchers traded in the covered market beneath - a 'Shambles' is a butcher's slaughterhouse. The Isle of Ely Assizes were held in the adjacent Shire Hall. Justice was administered either by public whipping at a pillory seen here on the roof, or at the whipping post and stocks on the ground floor. The old Shire Hall and Shambles were demolished in 1810, the town's pillory and stocks being relocated to the House of Correction in Gaol Lane. (Wisbech & Fenland Museum)

9.   In 1801 the old Butter Cross and Custom House in Bridge Street were demolished, the materials being incorporated into this imposing structure on the left. Under the superintendence of Thomas West the new Butter Cross was completed in 1804 at a cost of £2500. The Capital Burgesses moved their meetings from the Grammar School into these premises in 1810. Following the Municipal Act of 1835 the newly formed Wisbech Borough Council moved to Exchange Hall in North Brink. (Wisbech & Fenland Museum)

2: 1810-1819

10.   This 32ft high obelisk replaced an earlier Market Cross, reminding people of their religious obligations whilst transacting their daily business on the Market Place. It was said to be 'much blackened by bonfires which were kindled near its base when public rejoicings took place'. Mr Pope, a local builder and stonemason demolished the obelisk on Wednesday 17th April 1811. (Wisbech & Fenland Museum)

WISBECH TOWN BAILIFFS	
1810	William Jump
1811	Rev Abraham Jobson
1812	William Rayner
1813	Rev Jeremiah Jackson
1814	John Edes
1815	Hugh Jackson, Jnr
1816	Ralph Archbould
1817	Edward Ward
1818	H J Nicholls
1819	Robert Hardwicke

11.   An acute shortage of silver coinage prompted the Bank of England to issue 3s and 1s 6d Bank Tokens between 1811 and 1816. In 1804 using powerful machinery Boulton's Soho Mint in Birmingham had overstruck captured Spanish-American 'pieces of eight' to create a crown-size five shilling dollar coin. London's Mint had been situated in the Tower of London since the reign of Edward I but between 1810 and 1812 new Royal Mint premises, incorporating Boulton's machinery, were built on Tower Hill. (C.Cooke)

34mm

26mm

12.   The minting of tokens (unofficial coins) from 1811 onwards helped to alleviate the shortage of small change. Produced in silver, copper or bronze by private banks, local authorities and large companies their metallic worth was usually less than their face value. Local silver tokens were issued in Holbeach, King's Lynn, March and Peterborough. The British government tolerated these until the new Royal Mint had issued large quantities of small denominations.
(A.Ingram coll.))

13.   Thurloe's Mansion was built in 1656 for John Thurloe, Oliver Cromwell's Secretary of State, in the grounds of Wisbech Castle. Standing to the west of St Peter's Church the design closely resembled Thorpe Hall at Peterborough. Foundations of the 1478 Bishop's Palace, built on the Norman castle site, incorporated dungeons that once held Gunpowder Plot conspirators Robert Catesby and Francis Tresham. Local builder Joseph Medworth purchased the Mansion and Castle Estate from the Bishop of Ely in 1793 for £2305. (Fenland coll.)

14.   After demolishing some outbuildings around the mansion Joseph Medworth erected this Georgian crescent between 1793 and 1808. The Regency villa [centre] built by Medworth in 1816, incorporated materials from Thurloe's Mansion which he regrettably demolished. Window and door surrounds, three sets of gate piers together with stone features on the nearby Castle Lodge were all reclaimed from the Mansion. Following the death of Medworth and his heirs the Castle Estate was purchased at auction in 1864 for £1300 by William Peckover. (Fenland coll.)

15.   A George III shilling, one of a new set of silver coins issued by the Royal Mint on 17th February 1817. They were smaller and lighter than the coins they replaced and did not contain their intrinsic value of metal. The shilling had existed as a unit of reckoning since Saxon times. Henry VII introduced the silver coin, originally called a testoon, in the early 16th century. The term 'pounds, shillings and pence' defined British coinage until the introduction of decimalisation. (C.Cooke)

16.   James and Thomas Hill issued Wisbech Bank notes at their Bank House premises in South Brink, which opened in 1818. It stood almost opposite the home of Jonathan Peckover on North Brink. Hill's business, along with about 100 country banks, failed in the financial crisis of 1825. The pound unit of currency originated as a weight - 1lb of silver to mint 240 pennies - hence 240 old pennies equalled £1. The £ symbol is an abbreviation of Libra - the Latin word for pound. (Wisbech & Fenland Museum)

23mm

Proclamation of George the Fourth.

THE Capital Burgesses, Magistrates, Deputy Lieutenants, Clergy, and Gentlemen of the Town and Neighbourhood of Wisbech, will assemble on Wednesday next at ONE o'Clock at Noon, for the Purpose of meeting the Sheriff of the County, to publish and proclaim the High and Mighty PRINCE GEORGE the FOURTH, lawful and rightful King of these Realms and all the Dominions thereunto belonging.

Order of Procession.

Trumpeter on Horseback.

Petty Constable on Foot, with Staff. ⎰CHIEF CONSTABLE on Horseback,⎱ Petty Constable on Foot, with white Wand. with Staff.

Lieut. Col. WATSON of the Local Militia.

The Captains and other Officers of the Corps on Foot, by Twos.

The Junior Ensigns carrying the Colours of the Regiment.

The BAND.

The Sheriff's Officer with the Beadles of the Corporation on Foot, with white Wands.

The Clergy on Foot, in their Robes.

The SHERIFF,

Supported on the Right by the TOWN-BAILIFF, on the Left by J. EDES, Esq.

The Clerk of the Peace,

Supported on his Right by H. J. NICHOLLS, Esq. on the Left by the Rev. J. JACKSON.

Captain SWAINE, of the Navy,

Supported by W. RAYNER, Esq. on his Right, and Mr. E. WARD on his Left.

The other Magistrates of the Isle, and the Deputy Lieutenants of the County, by Threes.

The Gentlemen of the Town and Country on Horseback, by Threes.

The Petty Constables to be arranged by Distances on each side of the Procession

*** *The Procession is intended to be out of Mourning.*

☞ Such Gentlemen as are desirous of Dining, after the Proclamation, are requested to signify their Intentions at the Bar of the Rose and Crown Inn.

Wisbech, 7th Feb. 1820.   (J. WHITE, PRINTER.

III.   George, Prince of Wales had acted as Prince Regent since 11th February 1811 due to the deteriorating mental health of George III. On the death of his father, George IV acceded to the throne on 29th January 1820 and was crowned in Westminster Abbey on 19th July 1821. He had a number of mistresses before an arranged marriage in 1795 to Caroline of Brunswick. (Wisbech & Fenland Museum)

WISBECH TOWN BAILIFFS	
1820	W Swansborough
1821	W Watson FSA
1822	W Watson FSA
1823	Steed Girdlestone
1824	J R Weatherhead
1825	James Usill
1826	William Orton
1827	Charles Boucher
1828	Abraham Usill
1829	Henry James Nicholls

22mm

17.   Introduced in 1817 to replace the guinea, this sovereign was minted in 22 carat gold and valued at 20 shillings. A pound coin had first appeared in 1489 during the reign of Henry VII, the obverse design of a king enthroned in majesty giving rise to its name 'sovereign'. The classic portrayal of St George & Dragon appeared on the reverse of earlier sovereigns between 1817 and 1825 and from 1871 onwards. All sovereigns and half-sovereigns remain legal tender. (C.Cooke)

> ## PLEASURE BOAT TO LET
> EASIEST puller and fastest sailer in the river; lying at Sessions House steps. - Apply, AMOS FLANDERS.

18.   On the right stands the new Shire Hall, later called the Sessions House, erected in 1807 along South Brink. At a meeting in this building on Friday 24th June 1825 Dr Abraham Jobson, Vicar of St Peter's, offered £2000 towards the building of an overflow church or Chapel of Ease. Since 1801 the population of Wisbech had increased by almost 50% to around 7000 residents but the parish church could not accommodate the additional parishioners who wished to attend church services. (Wisbech & Fenland Museum)

Sir,

Our worthy vicar Dr Jobson, to whom you kindly sent the 7th Annual Report of the Society for promoting the Enlargement and Building of Churches & Chapels has empowered an intention of giving £2000 towards building an additional Church or Chapel in this town, which has stimulated his parishioners to give their aid towards accomplishing an object so desirable. The population of Wisbech consists of about 7,000 and although very considerable improvements and a large sum of money has been expended in recent accommodations the church cannot be made capable of holding more than about sixteen hundred. Our intention is to build an additional church or chapel on so economical a plan, as may be, to hold about 1200. It is the Doctor's thought that the area of the floor should be equipped for free lettings, and the gallery for seats which may be let to inhabitants, who may advance the money. We have not yet had any General Meeting of the Parishioners but we are in hopes that we shall be able to raise the money required, without applying to any public fund. The Doctor however wished me to write first to you, conceiving you may be enabled to give me some useful information, as to what sort of plan you would recommend for me to pursue. About what expense will be required for a plain Brick Edifice. He thinks you probably would have the kindness to grant me the loan of some plans, which shall be faithfully returned. What you think, should be the dimensions of such a church to contain about 1200; with any other particulars you may think useful. Request to apologize for the trouble I have given you.

*I have the honour to be
Sir your most obedient and
humble servant
Wm Watson*

*Wisbech
24th June 1825*

IV.   In this letter to W.J.Nobber, Secretary to the Church Building Society, William Watson, High Bailiff of the Isle of Ely, writes *In respect of building an additional Church or Chapel at Wisbech*. In 1818 Parliament had passed the Church Building Act which created 'The Society for Promoting the Enlargement and Building of Churches & Chapels'. Backed by a Tory government grant of £6 million the Society's role was *to raise funds for, and encourage the repair or building of, parish churches, and to offer informed advice.* If the requested plans were loaned they may not have been returned as faithfully promised, as this letter was the only document to remain in their files. (Lambeth Palace Library)

27mm

19. Originally a silver coin, the copper halfpenny had been introduced in the reign of Charles II. Between 1685 and 1690 during the reigns of James II and William & Mary the halfpenny had been minted in tin to help the Cornish tin industry. The copper coins of George IV depict a seated Britannia facing right, a tradition that continued on the reverse [tail] side of all half-pennies until 1936. (C.Cooke)

20. William Swans-borough, Churchwarden at St Peter's and former Town Bailiff, prepared these draft plans for a rectangular Chapel to hold about 1200 people. Public meetings were called to consider an eligible plan, and after much consideration, that of an octagon shape was eventually adopted. The Wisbech Chapel of Ease Act received its Royal Assent on 14th June 1827. Pews in the tiered gallery were reserved through the sale of £50 shares, whilst those on the ground floor remained free.
(Syndics of Cambridge University Library)

21.   Thomas Pattison Holmes, seen here in later life, laid the foundation stone of the Octagon Church on behalf of an ailing Dr Jobson on Monday 6th August 1827. William Watson's 1827 History of Wisbech recorded that he *offered up in few words an appropriate prayer, invoking the favour of Heaven on the undertaking, and calling upon Almighty God, for the sake of his son Jesus Christ our Lord, to prosper it with his especial blessing.* The Act stipulated that Abraham Jobson would nominate the first minister of the Chapel of Ease, therefore on 7th September 1830 he appointed his nephew Thomas Holmes. Dr Jobson passed away on 13th December 1830 aged 84, with the newly completed Octagon Church standing as his memorial. (Wisbech & Fenland Museum)

V.   Prince William Henry, third son of George III, ascended to the throne on 26th June 1830 following the death of his eldest brother George IV. Married to Adelaide of Saxe-Coburg in July 1818 William IV was crowned on 8th September 1831. (Wisbech & Fenland Museum)

WISBECH
Coronation Festival.

STEWARDS.

WILLIAM WATSON, Esq.	ALEXANDER FRASER, Esq. M.D.
T. S. WATSON, Esq. Town Bailiff	CHARLES METCALFE, Esq.
Rev. H. FARDELL, Vicar	ISAAC JECKS, Esq.
ROBERT HARDWICKE, Esq. M.D.	JAMES USILL. Esq.
H. J. NICHOLLS, Esq.	R. F. PATE, Esq.
JONATHAN PECKOVER, Esq.	WILLIAM ORTON, Esq.

Presidents.

Rev. R. J. King	Mr. Trevor
Rev. T. P. Holmes	Dr. Stuart
Rev. J. R. Major	Mr. H. Morton
Rev. J. Cookson	Mr. J. Pope
Mr. W. Jecks	Mr. M. Leach
Mr. N. Walker	Mr. R. Clarke
Mr. C. Jecks	Mr. J. Smith
Mr. Denston	Mr. T. Dawbarn
Mr. A. Peckover	Mr. T. Hall
Mr. C. Metcalfe, Jun.	Mr. T. Moore
Mr. A. Usill	Mr. R. C. Life
Mr. Weatherhead	Mr. W. Stevens
Mr. E. Jackson	Mr. J. Hardy
Lieut Schultz, R. N.	Mr. H. Ollard
Mr. H. M. Usill	

Vice-Presidents.

Mr. Rumball	Mr. Isley
Mr. J. Leach	Mr. J. Harrison
Mr. D. Fardell	Mr. T. Pattrick
Mr. R. Adams	Mr. Sallabank
Mr. J. Adams	Mr. J. Goward
Mr. J. Lilley	Mr. R. Baxter
Mr. W. Reeve	Mr W. Wales
Mr. W. P. Bays	Mr. F. Fawssett
Mr. R. Watts	Mr. W. Grounds
Mr. R. Freeman	Mr. Huckbody
Mr. J. C. Baker	Mr. C. Huckbody
Mr. J. Cripps	Mr. W. Springfield
Mr. T. Wright	Mr. W. Woollard
Mr. M. H. Osborne	Mr. W. Beatley.
Mr. J. Groom	

A MEETING of the above Presidents and Vice-Presidents will be held at the Town Hall, on WEDNESDAY Afternoon, at Four o'Clock precisely.---Persons willing to undertake the Duties of Carvers and Assistants, are requested to send in their Names to the Committee as soon as possible, and to attend at the Town Hall at the above mentioned hour, to receive their Ticket of Appointment and Instructions.

By Order of the Committee,

T. S. WATSON, *Chairman.*

Committee Room, Town Hall, Tuesday
Afternoon, September 6th, 1831.

(H. & J. Leach, Printers, Wisbech.

22.   Built of yellow brick, faced in some parts with Portland stone and plaster, the Octagon Church stood 88ft high x 102ft long, with an interior diagonal diameter of about 60ft. Inside the south porch hung a single bidding bell resembling an up-turned pudding basin, whilst stairs either side of the porch led up to the tiered gallery. The lantern's design was based on Ely Cathedral lantern but there the similarity ended. The sides of the Octagon's lantern were slate, window frames of iron, the crockets [decorative features] of composition, and the wooden pinnacles were coated with plaster. This 26ft high structure was merely fastened to the roof with nails. (Syndics of Cambridge University Library)

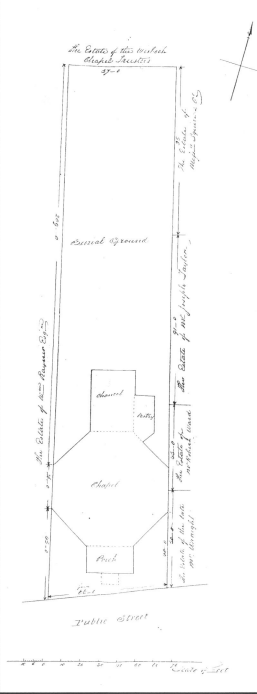

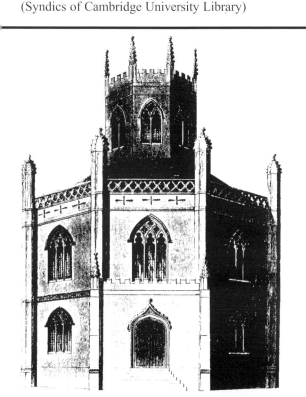

A Ground Plan of the Site of the Chapel of Ease, lately erected at Wisbech St Peters in the Diocese and Isle of Ely and of the Burial Ground adjoining

by. W Swanborough

Nov 26 1830

23.   William IV silver half-crowns were only minted for general circulation between 1834 and 1837. Introduced as a gold coin by Henry VIII, half-crowns were first minted in silver by Edward VI in 1551. During William IVs short reign only three million half-crowns were produced, compared to nine million for George IV. There were no William IV crown coins in general circulation although a few special 'proof' coins were minted in 1831 and 1834. (C.Cooke)

32mm

24.   Princess Victoria had ridden in a horse-drawn closed carriage along this road when she visited Wisbech on Tuesday 22nd September 1835. The Royal Party, escorted by the Corporation on horseback, travelled along a crowded North Brink to the Town Hall where the horses were changed. Through the open carriage window Victoria bowed pleasantly to acknowledge the cheering crowds as her entourage proceeded slowly over the Stone Bridge and along High Street for a brief stop at the Rose & Crown Hotel. (Fenland coll.)

25.   At the Canal Sluice, situated close beside this three-storey brewery, three cheers were given and the band played the National Anthem. Victoria, wearing a pink drawn bonnet and accompanied by her mother, the Duchess of Kent, then continued her journey to Holkham Hall. In her journal Victoria recalled *we were delayed there, I should think upwards of a 1/4 of an hour on account of the crowd and confusion which were both very great. There was great pushing and squeezing.* (Fenland coll.)

Wisbech & Ely

UNION

Packet Boat

Edward Stevens, *Owner*, John Lee, *Master.*

THE Public are most respectfully informed that the above Boat leaves Wisbech every Monday Morning, at Seven o'Clock, from the Canal Sluice, for the Conveyance of Goods and Passengers through Elm, Emneth, Outwell, Nordelph, Salter's Lode, Denver Sluice, Littleport, to Ely, where it arrives the same Afternoon; whence Goods may be quickly forwarded to Soham, Fordham, Downham in the Isle, Stretham, Milton, Waterbeach, Wilburton, Haddenham, Witchford, Witcham, Coveney, Sutton, Mepal, Cambridge, Newmarket, Bury, and all other places adjacent. The Packet Boat will leave Ely every Friday Morning, at Eight o'Clock, from the New Quay, and arrive at Wisbech the same Afternoon, when Goods may be forwarded the following day, to Guyhirn, Wisbech St. Mary's, Parson Drove, Leverington, Newton, Tydd St. Giles, Tydd St. Mary's, Sutton St. Edmund's, Long Sutton, Gedney, Fleet, Holbeach, Spalding, Boston, March, Chatteris, &c.

The greatest care will be taken of the Goods entrusted to the Master, and the delivery punctually attended to.

☞ Small Parcels may be left to the care of Mr. W. STEVENS, Draper, York Row, Wisbech.

Wisbech, 12th July, 1831.

(H. & J. Leach, Printers, Wisbech

26.   Upon her arrival in Wisbech Henry Leach the Town Bailiff had presented the 16-year-old Princess Victoria with an inscribed copy of William Watson's 1827 History of Wisbech. Victoria ascended to the throne on 20th June 1837 following the death of her uncle William IV, and in February 1840 married Prince Albert. Some years later, following a request by the Mayor James Fraser, her majesty sent an inscribed engraving as a memento of her visit to Wisbech. (Wisbech & Fenland Museum)

27.   First published on 3rd September 1836 and backed by Wisbech banker James Hill 'to help forward the cause of humanity', *The Star in the East* masthead proclaimed *The Truth, the whole truth, and nothing but the truth.* In 1835 James had married Caroline Southwood Smith and on 3rd December 1838 she gave birth to her third daughter, Octavia. Following his second bankruptcy publication of the paper ceased in May 1840 and the family moved to Epping. (Wisbech & Fenland Museum)

28.   William IV reintroduced the groat or fourpenny piece for general circulation in 1836. First

16mm

introduced by Edward I in 1279 the name originated from the French word 'gros' meaning great or thick. The last groat for general circulation was minted in 1855, but in 1888 groats with Queen Victoria's Jubilee Head were produced for use in British Guiana. Silver groats continued to be minted as Maundy Money, whilst the threat of receiving 'a fourpenny one' remained in the English language. (C.Cooke)

29.   A Dinner on Wisbech Market Place, attended by 5000 people, celebrated the Coronation of Queen Victoria on Thursday 28th June 1838. The bill of fare included 4176lbs of meat, 3654lbs of potatoes, and 542 x 7lb puddings, of which 56 were cooked at the Old Workhouse. The platform party, led by Mayor Thomas Dawbarn, included Hugh Jackson (Clerk of the Peace), William Peckover (Banker), and Rev T.P.Holmes (Octagon Church). The day's festivities on the Market Place concluded with a fireworks display. (A.Ingram collection)

REGULATIONS FOR THE FESTIVAL

On *THURSDAY the 28th day of JUNE*, 1838,

IN CELEBRATION OF

THE CORONATION OF QUEEN VICTORIA.

The Church Bells will ring at Seven and Eleven o'clock in the Morning. At Half-past Twelve o'clock the Bells will again ring, at which time precisely the Inhabitants of the Town are to assemble at the places specified in their respective Tickets, viz.

First Division	For Market Place, Church Lane, Ship Lane, and adjoining Alleys	Ship Lane.
Second Division ..	For the Horse Fair	Horse Fair.
Third Division	For the South Brink and Deadman's Lane	Yorke Row.
Fourth Division	For the North Brink and the Old Market............................	Facing the Vine.
Fifth Division	For Trafalgar Row, Lynn Road, and East Field	Sluice Bridge.
Sixth Division	For the South end of Timber Market, Elm Street, New Wisbech, and beyond the Ferry Boat	Hill facing the Ferry Boat.
Seventh Division..	For the North part of Timber Market between the Church Yard and the Ferry Boat	Opening facing the Wheat Sheaf.

They will there find ready to receive them, the Presidents and Vice-Presidents of their respective Tables, who will head their own Companies, and with as little delay as possible proceed to the Market Place. The President of the first Table of each Division will proceed first ; the next Table in rotation after him, and so on, till all are occupied. There will be at the head of every Table a Label corresponding with the Ticket of the Division and the number of the Table upon it. Each President will conduct his Company to the proper Table, where the Carvers will be ready seated, and the Company will take their seats in the intermediate spaces. The Carvers are requested to be in their respective places by Half-past Twelve o'clock precisely.

17mm

14mm

16mm

30.   Half-farthings (top left) introduced by George IV in 1828 for use in Ceylon were minted between 1839 and 1856 for general circulation in Great Britain. Over six million quarter-farthings (top right) were manufactured in copper between 1839 and 1853 for use in Ceylon. Even third-farthings (left) originally produced for use in Malta, were minted for general circulation during Victoria's reign. (C.Cooke)

IMPORTANT NOTICE!!

REID *v.* GARDINER.

The Inhabitants of Wisbech must be highly gratified to be informed that the

Excessive Damages--

"ONE FARTHING"

Obtained in this Notorious Action, will be spent in BREAD, to be given to the Poor during the ensuing Winter, should the Weather be so severe as to demand such an act of disinterested Benevolence.

The great Liberality of the Plaintiff towards the Poor generally cannot now be questioned.

GODDARD, Printer, Wisbeach.

31.   A letter from Samuel Buckle to Robert Dawbarn, dated 28th November 1840, regarding a window in the George & Dragon stable. This letter carries a Penny Black stamp, the world's first adhesive postage stamp, which had come into use on 6th May 1840. Pigot's Cambridgeshire Directory for 1839 stated that in Wisbech *letters from London and all parts arrive every morning at eleven minutes past seven, and are despatched every evening at twenty-two minutes before seven. The box closes a quarter of an hour before the despatch of the mails.* The postmaster John Goward had his office in Union Street in premises later occupied by the Wisbech Advertiser. (S.Benstead collection)

32.   Richard Young was born at Scarning in Norfolk on 22nd March 1809. At the age of 28 he was appointed Keeper of the North Level Sea Sluice and Surveyor of the North Level Main Drain, which had been completed in 1834. In 1837 he purchased the *Elizabeth Huddleston*, the first of 43 vessels he was to own over the years. Richard Young was elected as a Borough Councillor in November 1855 and Mayor of Wisbech three years later, a post he held for five consecutive years until 1863. (L.Monaghan)

WISBECH MAYORS	
1840	Thomas Steed Watson
1841	Thomas Steer
1842	James Usill
1843	Charles Metcalfe, Jnr
1844	John Whitsed
1845	William Stevens
1846	William Stevens
1847	Henry Leach
1848	William Stevens
1849	Henry William Ward

33. The 18 ton paddle steamer *Don* sailing up river was jointly owned by coal merchant Barnabas Hickson, chemist William Grounds, and former Town Bailiff Harley Matthew Usill. On 5th December 1854 they sold the vessel to local coal merchant and ship owner Richard Young. Webster's wooden post mill is to the right of the Octagon, with Leach's eight-sail mill on the left.
(Lilian Ream Exhibition Gallery)

34. Three figures stand outside the new Corporation crane and warehouse along Nene Quay. Between 1829 and 1840 trade through Wisbech Port had doubled to 109,885 tons. The Mayor, Dr John Whitsed, had laid the foundation stone for this fine building in 1845. Situated beside the entrance to Wisbech Canal this building, which also served as a mortuary, was later replaced by a corrugated iron structure. (Fenland coll.)

35.   The first edition of *The Wisbech Advertiser* was published on Saturday 2nd August 1845. This four-page monthly newspaper was printed and published by John Gardiner at his office, next to the New Inn in Union Street. In the editorial he noted that *many have urged the expediency of a weekly issue.* Following the abolition of advertisement duty in 1853 and stamp duty in 1855 the paper appeared weekly from June 1855. In January 1887 it was increased to eight pages and renamed *Isle of Ely and Wisbech Advertiser.* (A.Ingram collection)

36.   Within fifteen years the Octagon's original lantern had become unsafe due to its flimsy construction. In 1846 local architect J.C.Buckler designed this replacement, described by Walker & Craddock as *merely a battlement perforated with quatrefoils, and surmounted with pinnacles, looking like a coronet on the edifice.* In July 1835 the Wisbech Museum collection had been established in two rented rooms behind George Snarey's shop in the Old Market. Captain Schultz RN, the first curator, was succeeded in 1841 by Thomas Foster who held the post until 1874. (Fenland coll.)

37.   The original museum building in Old Market had become inadequate to house a growing collection; therefore these new museum premises were constructed. Designed by J.C.Buckler, and depicted here in a water-colour by Algernon Peckover, this was one of the first purpose-built museum buildings in the country. Major General Sir Harry Smith, a native of Whittlesey, opened The Wisbech and Fenland Museum on Tuesday 27th July 1847. (Margaret Cave collection)

38.   Wisbech's most famous son, Thomas Clarkson, passed away on Saturday 26th September 1846 at Playford Hall, near Ipswich. Thomas was born on 28th March 1760 at Wisbech Grammar School, where his father Rev John Clarkson was headmaster. His obsession with the abolition of slavery began at St John's College, Cambridge whilst researching his Latin essay on 'The Slavery and Commerce of the Human Species'. He subsequently gathered information on the slave trade that was presented before Parliament by another abolitionist William Wilberforce MP. In his obituary *The Times* remarked *Clarkson was the back-bone of the anti-slavery cause.* (Wisbech & Fenland Museum)

39.   Josiah Rumball laid the foundation stone for this General Cemetery chapel, designed by William Adams, on 28th April 1848. This former garden covering 3.5 acres off Leverington Road was established as a cemetery in 1836, primarily for non-conformists. Purchased from Mr Josiah Bland for £950, the new owners formed the Wisbech General Cemetery Company in 1841. A total of 210 shares were offered at £5 each with 21 of the shareholders being appointed trustees. The first interment took place on Friday 25th March 1836 when Robert Catliff, the infant son of William and Anne Catliff, was laid to rest. (Fenland coll.)

40.   The New Burial Ground in King's
Walk had opened in 1832 to relieve the
overcrowded churchyard at St Peter's.
However a national Cholera epidemic
reached Wisbech that year and 42 victims
were buried here away from the town centre.
In 1849 the epidemic claimed 47 victims in
Wisbech, where the average life expectancy
of just 27 years was even lower than in
London. Professor Willis of Cambridge
designed this burial-ground chapel, 30ft long
by 16ft wide, with the foundation stone being
laid by the Countess of Hardwicke on
Thursday 17th August 1843. Although
officially closed for interments in 1881 when
the Borough Cemetery opened in Mount
Pleasant, family plots in this burial-ground
continued to be used.
(Fenland coll.)

A SPECIAL

FORM OF PRAYER

TO BE USED

In all Churches and Chapels throughout those
Parts of the United Kingdom called ENGLAND
and IRELAND, instead of the PRAYER used during
any TIME of COMMON PLAGUE or SICKNESS,

ON SUNDAY THE SIXTEENTH OF SEPTEMBER;

And to be continued during the Prevalence of the
Cholera in this Country ; for obtaining Pardon
of our Sins ; and, particularly, for beseeching
God to remove from us that grievous Disease
with which many Places in this Kingdom are
now visited.

By Her Majesty's Special Command.

LONDON:
Printed by GEORGE EDWARD EYRE and WILLIAM SPOTTISWOODE,
Printers to the Queen's most Excellent Majesty.
1849.

41.   Railway powers were obtained in 1849 for this iron bridge to cross the River Nene from The Low on North Brink. In The Woodlands on South Brink lived Rev T.P.Holmes, incumbent of the Octagon Church. His red brick house with its fine Dutch gable end stood alongside the proposed bridge site. In 1846 a dozen projected railway lines through Wisbech had heralded the arrival of 'Railway Mania'. Wisbech Corporation expressed strong objections to any railway crossing the River Nene and obstructing navigation. The bridge was actually cast, but never erected. (Wisbech & Fenland Museum)

42.   In 1849 a silver two-shilling piece known as a florin was introduced. This name originated from the Latin 'fiorino' meaning flower, for florins first minted in Florence included a lily design. Between 1851 and 1887 the florin's date was given in Roman numerals, which had first appeared on English coins during the reign of Edward VI. Half-crowns were not minted for circulation between 1851 and 1873, allowing the public time to accept the new florin coin. Its issue was a proposed step towards decimalisation for the florin's reverse design included the inscription one tenth of a pound. (C.Cooke)

30mm

WISBECH MAYORS	
1850	John Whitsed
1851	Henry Morton
1852	James Edward Fraser
1853	Harley M Usill
1854	Robert Wherry
1855	James Edward Fraser
1856	Thomas Steed Watson
1857	Thomas Steed Watson
1858	Richard Young
1858	Richard Young

VI.   'Plan of the Town of Wisbech with New Walsoken from the actual survey by Frederick J Utting. October 1850' from a photograph by Samuel Smith. (Wisbech & Fenland Museum)

43.   This view of Hill House in Upper Hill Street is one of the earliest photographs of Wisbech. The photographer, Thomas Craddock, was joint author with Neil Walker of the 1849 History of Wisbech and his photographs were exhibited in the Crystal Palace Great Exhibition of 1851. Prince Albert, who had organised the exhibition, later requested a copy of Craddock's photograph of Ely Cathedral for the Royal Collection. Thomas Craddock subsequently became Professor of Literature at Queen's College, Liverpool and died aged 82 on 9th April 1893. (Wisbech & Fenland Museum)

44.   This photograph by Thomas Craddock of Webster's Mill includes Samuel Smith sitting by the wall. Born at Tydd St Giles on Sunday 28th February 1802 Samuel followed his elder brother Joseph to Nottingham to serve an apprenticeship in the textile trade. There he married the boss's daughter Myra, before moving to March around 1830 to join his brother John as a timber merchant. Samuel and Myra lived in Whittle End, March with their two daughters but by about 1847 were able to retire to Leverington, still in their forties. (Lilian Ream Exhibition Gallery)

45.   The Smiths moved into Malvern House where Samuel took up photography, with Thomas Craddock probably acting as his tutor. Only 13 years after the photographic negative had been invented by Fox Talbot, Smith and Craddock using the 'calotype' process photographed Fenland towns and villages. After preparing a new batch of waxed paper plates, measuring approximately 8in x 10in, Smith photographed the exterior of his house. By taking this standard test subject and then processing the plate he could calculate the exposure time required for the remaining plates. (Wisbech & Fenland Museum)

46.   This elegant stone bridge of 1758 replaced a succession of wooden bridges, the last being erected in 1637. Following heavy rainfall in November 1852 the bridge foundations were eroded by water rushing through 'The Throttle' - the narrow channel and sharp curve by the bridge. The Nene Valley Commissioners had already proposed replacing this bridge in their Drainage Act of 1852. The dormer window visible above the balustrades belonged to the White Lion Hotel, rebuilt in 1883. (Wisbech & Fenland Museum)

47   Jonathan Peckover moved from Fakenham to Wisbech in 1777 where he opened a draper's shop here in the High Street. In 1781 he founded the Wisbech Literary Society which met a few doors along in the Rose & Crown Hotel on the right. Soon this trusted Quaker began looking after some of his customer's gold and silver coins for a small fee, leading to the establishment of the first official Wisbech bank in 1782. By 1794 Jonathan and his family were able to move into the best house in town, later known as Bank House. (G.Drew collection)

48.   Hailed as one of the most perfect Georgian streets in England, the North Brink contained Bank House, described as the showpiece of Wisbech. To its left was the single-storey Wisbech & Lincolnshire Bank erected by Jonathan Peckover in 1800 to replace the High Street premises. Algernon Peckover designed Wisteria House with its stepped Jacobean gables on the extreme left, whilst in the centre stands an early 18th century warehouse with its pantiled roof. The artist J.C.Sammons had clambered down the riverbank to frame this view of North Brink beneath the elliptical arch of the stone bridge. (Fenland coll.)

49.   Silver 3d pieces were minted for general circulation throughout the reign of Queen Victoria. In William IVs reign they had only been produced for use in the West Indies. Introduced by Edward VI circa 1551, the silver 3d had been included in the annual Maundy Money distribution by the monarch since the reign of Charles II. The age-old tradition of including silver three-penny bits in the Christmas pudding mix was said to bring wealth, health and happiness to whoever found the coin in their dish. (C.Cooke)

17mm

50.   Exchange Hall, built in 1811 by Joseph Medworth, is seen here on the right in 1853. Originally consisting of two rooms raised upon five open arches, the ground floor was fitted out as a corn exchange with stalls let at three guineas a year. In 1831 the ground floor was re-let for an annual rent of one sovereign on condition that the room was converted for public meetings and exhibitions. On 29th July 1858 a new corn exchange began trading behind the Exchange Hall, these central arches being opened up to provide access. Rev Charles Haddon Spurgeon, the Baptist evangelist, preached at the Corn Exchange on 1st October 1863 to an estimated audience of 2000. (Wisbech & Fenland Museum)

51.   In February 1854 the Nene Valley Commissioners commenced piling the riverbanks from Wisbech Bridge to Horseshoe Corner, close by Samuel Smith's home. The six pile drivers seen here lining Nene Parade are powered by a small steam engine just visible by the ship's bow. Cargo destined for inland wharves would be transferred to shallow draft Fen lighters that could navigate the extensive inland waterways system. (Wisbech & Fenland Museum)

52.   Horses had previously been used to haul imported timber up the muddy riverbank along Nene Parade, but following completion of the piling work this travelling crane on the left was erected to unload the ships. Samuel Smith has taken this photograph from Webster's Mill, with the four-sail Brewin's Mill in Timber Market visible on the horizon. (Wisbech & Fenland Museum)

53.   John Goward is probably one of the two men standing outside the Post Office (right) in this Samuel Smith photograph dated Wednesday 6th September 1854. These buildings were demolished shortly after the photograph had been taken. The Post Office moved to the South Brink house formerly occupied by banker James Hill. By 1865 pillar letterboxes, situated in Timber Market and the Sluice, were cleared three times a day and once on Sundays. Mr Goward had succeeded his mother as Postmaster of Wisbech in 1830, and was followed by his son John Goward in 1884.
(Wisbech & Fenland Museum)

54.   The Old Workhouse in Albion Place, photographed on Monday 4th September 1854. This building was erected under a 1722 Act but failed to meet the more stringent conditions in the 1835 Poor Law Act. Inmates were therefore transferred to the new Union Workhouse in Lynn Road, with the Old Workhouse being sold for £1700. A picturesque bell and clock turret, bearing the date 1722 had been removed when the building was divided into these smaller premises. The Custom House [centre] had previously been located in the Butter Cross which was demolished in 1856.
(Wisbech & Fenland Museum)

55.	Demolition work on the stone bridge commenced in early 1855 and by Thursday 22nd March only the barest minimum of stonework remained. At 5pm that day workmen began breaking blocks of stone on the north side of the bridge and three hours later about 100 tons of masonry fell into the river. The foundation stone of 1758 bearing a commemorative plaque was donated to Wisbech Museum. (Wisbech & Fenland Museum)

56.	A temporary wooden bridge was completed in November 1854 to allow passage across the river. This photograph, taken from Bank House and dated Wednesday 17th September 1856, includes the new Iron Bridge under construction. The Admiralty insisted that a replacement bridge should be moveable to allow ships to sail up the River Nene to Peterborough. A number of properties on Cornhill and Bridge Street, including the Butter Cross, had already been demolished as part of the scheme. (Wisbech & Fenland Museum)

57.   Robert Stephenson was consultant engineer for this structure, which at 150ft long x 40ft wide x 8ft high was described as the largest opening bridge in the world. The Mayor J.E.Fraser laid the Iron Bridge foundation stone on 11th April 1856. The hydraulic mechanism, operated by about six men in the corrugated iron tower on South Brink, would lift the bridge whilst chains moved the structure. Two-thirds of the bridge length, pivoting by the bank, would swing over the river to South Brink, whilst the remaining weighted length acting as ballast. (Wisbech & Fenland Museum)

58.   At 6am on 3rd November 1857, with the
Mayor and Corporation looking on, the bridge
was successfully swung open for the first time.
At the formal opening ceremony just before noon
on Monday 9th November Thomas Steed Watson
was driven across in his carriage to the Town
Hall, where he was re-elected Mayor. He was
followed by Richard Young who drove his
carriage across, and Robert Dawbarn who rode
on horseback. The photographic negative had
been invented in 1839 but local newspapers
continued to use engravings for their illustrations
throughout the 19th century.
(Lilian Ream Exhibition Gallery)

59.   Between 1856 and 1857 extensive
restoration work took place at St Peter's Church
under the direction of Sir George Gilbert Scott.
This view facing Church Terrace shows the
bricked-up east window of the south Chancel.
Restoration work in 1856 revealed a
Perpendicular window behind the brickwork,
whilst sympathetic Victorian builders replaced the
Decorated east window of the north chancel with
one in a 14th century style.
(Fenland coll.)

←

60.   This imposing St Peter's Church tower dates from around 1530; replacing the original tower that had collapsed into the church nave around 1450. Sturdy pillars and a spiral staircase, remnants from the Norman tower flank the west door beside the lamppost. The tower seen here houses a unique peal of 10 bells, cast by William Dobson of Downham Market and inaugurated on 19th December 1823. Legend has it that no clock was installed on the east face as the residents of Walsoken refused to subscribe to the timepiece! (Wisbech & Fenland Museum)

61.   This first Wisbech Gas Works was constructed in Leverington Road during 1832, with George Marshall becoming the resident manager. Wisbech Corporation took out a 21-year contract with the Yorkshire owner, Mr Malam, to supply gas to the town. The streets of Wisbech were lit by 95 full lamps and 72 half lamps, described as 'union jets', at a cost of £280 per annum. Initially very few private houses installed gas lighting because of its high cost, whilst traders complained about interrupted supplies. Local businessmen formed The Wisbech Gas Light and Coke Company in 1858 and bought out Mr Malam in September 1859. (Wisbech & Fenland Museum)

WISBECH
VOLUNTEER
RIFLE CORPS.

At a Committee Meeting held in the TOWN HALL, (this day) the following Resolutions were passed :--

1st.---That Messrs. Young, Shelford, Ward and Gapp, be appointed a Sub-committee to report upon the first, and probable annual expense of establishing and supporting the Corps. To select the most appropriate spot for practice. To obtain pattern and estimate of Arms and Uniform. To canvas for Volunteers, and to obtain every information in their power, to be laid before the General Committee at the next meeting.

2nd.---That each member of the Rifle Corps may find his own outfit according to the pattern selected by the Committee; but, if any member should not wish to procure his outfit at his own expense, the Committee will guarantee that the whole amount required of him shall not exceed EIGHT POUNDS (including rifle), and the Sub-committee shall have power to reduce this sum if found expedient.

RICHD. YOUNG,
CHAIRMAN.

Wisbech, June 11, 1859.

GARDINER & CO., MACHINE PRINTERS, WISBECH.

VII.   In 1859 the Prime Minister Lord Palmerston established a Volunteer Movement to defend Britain against a possible threat of invasion by Napoleon III. On 24th January 1860 the Mayoress Mrs Richard Young formally presented the Wisbech Volunteer Rifle Corps, dressed in new Lincoln green uniforms, with their colours and bugle. Napoleon III was a nephew of Napoleon Bonaparte who was defeated by the Duke of Wellington in 1815. His Breakfast Service was captured on the battlefield of Waterloo and subsequently bequeathed to Wisbech Museum by Rev Chauncy Hare Townshend. (Wisbech & Fenland Museum)

62.	The National Provincial Bank, a finely detailed classical building on Cornhill, photographed circa 1860. The Wisbech branch opened on 12th August 1834 in leased premises on this site, with manager A.P.MacEwen on a salary of £300 per annum. The original building was demolished circa 1850 to be replaced by this structure in stone and yellow brick. It was probably designed by John Gibson who was also responsible for the company's banks in Bury St Edmunds and Peterborough. (NatWest)

63.   This well-known Victorian 'bun' penny design was introduced in 1860; the nickname derived from her hairstyle. The first penny coin had been minted in silver during the 8th century and was based on the Roman 'denarius', hence the abbreviation '1d'. Minted in bronze the bun penny replaced the copper pennies introduced by George III in 1806, though all bronze coins were referred to as 'coppers'. This young portrait of the Queen appeared on all bronze coins up to 1894, by which time Victoria was 75 years old! (C.Cooke)

31mm

64.   This is the earliest known Wisbech railway photograph, dated Saturday 18th April 1863, and probably taken by local photographer Edward Johnson. The Prince and Princess of Wales are returning to London on the Great Eastern Railway after spending their honeymoon at Sandringham. The couple had stopped their train at Wisbech allowing the townsfolk to pass on their loyal greetings, following representations by the Mayor Richard Young. On 3rd January 1868 he was appointed a Director by the GER who named their 240ft paddle steamer *Richard Young* in 1871.
(Lilian Ream Exhibition Gallery)

65.   Celebrations on the Market Place as clean water finally arrived in Wisbech on Friday 22nd September 1865. The town had lacked both clean drinking water and proper sanitary conditions, residents previously obtaining their water from the River, Canal, and public pumps. Following the Wisbech cholera epidemics of 1848 and 1849 the Corporation adopted the Public Health Act of 1848. However public financial constraints delayed full implementation until George Dawbarn formed the private Wisbech Waterworks Company in 1864. Water purchased from Mr Makemead's spring at Marham flowed along a nine-inch pipe to Wisbech, via the pumping station at Wiggenhall St Germans. At first supplies were limited to daytime, a serious drawback for the local Fire Brigade, but from 1877 there was a continuous flow. (G.Drew collection)

A comprehensive history of Wisbech railways can be found in the companion volume *Branch Lines around Wisbech.*

66.   William Ellis was born in London on 29th August 1794, but three years later his family moved to Wisbech and rented a cottage on the Horse Fair. William returned to London aged 18 to work as a nurseryman for Mr Sangster, a steadfast Christian attending the Kingsland Baptist Chapel. William became a Sunday school teacher and later trained with the London Missionary Society. With no formal education this 'Wisbech working man' came to be hailed as a great Christian missionary and explorer in the South Sea Islands. He later represented the LMS in Madagascar where he wrote the first History of Madagascar and took the earliest photographs of the island. On returning to England in 1867 his first lecture was to the Working Mens Institute in Wisbech. He died at Hoddesdon in Hertfordshire on 9th June 1872 aged 77. (Wisbech & Fenland Museum)

67.   Jonathan Peckover, grandson of Jonathan the first Peckover banker, founded this Working Men's Club and Institute in 1864 for the local Temperance Movement. By 1867 the membership of 267 had outgrown their hired room in Upper Hill Street and these premises were purchased. Algernon Peckover laid the foundation stone for a new Lecture Hall in 1871, then two years later work commenced on a Gymnasium. An increasing number of clubs and societies began using the premises that included reading, smoking and club rooms. The Institute's emblem bore the legend Labour, Learning, Love and by 1898 the membership had grown to 1200 with a lending library containing 16,000 books.
(Wisbech & Fenland Museum)

68.   Richard Young stood for the 1865 Parliamentary Elections as a Liberal. He won a seat, and together with two Conservatives, who were returned unopposed, they represented the Cambridgeshire Constituency. He lost his seat in the 1868 election by just 40 votes to another Liberal, the Rt Hon Henry Brand. The following year he lost a King's Lynn by-election by just 19 votes to the Conservative candidate Lord Claud Hamilton, who became chairman of the Great Eastern Railway in 1893. (Wisbech & Fenland Museum)

69.   The Wesleyan Methodist chapel in The Crescent, opened in 1803 for a congregation that originally met in a barn. This chapel was enlarged in 1835 at a cost of £1200 to increase its seating capacity to five hundred. In February 1863 the United Methodist Free Church, which had seceded from the Wesleyan Methodists in 1857, opened their Methodist Free Church in Little Church Street. The Primitive Methodists, who had worshipped in Wisbech since 1824, opened their new chapel on Church Terrace in April 1869. In the 19th century membership of the Methodist movement in England and Wales increased from 91,825 to 732,668. (G.Drew collection)

70.   Designed by Mr Bassett-Smith in the Early English style, St Augustine's church was erected for around £4000 on the corner of Lynn Road and Monica Road. This is the earliest photograph of St Augustine's, taken shortly after completion. The Bishop of Ely conducted the consecration service on Tuesday 11th May 1869 and Rev A.J.Perry began serving an ecclesiastical parish population of 4000. The Leverington Rectory Act of August 1871 had included provision for a vicarage and endowment for this newly established parish, formed from the civil parishes of Wisbech St Peter and Leverington.
(Wisbech & Fenland Museum)

71.   Rev   C.H.Townshend bequeathed   this   original manuscript of *Great Expectations* by Charles Dickens to Wisbech Museum in 1869, along with his extensive collection of ceramics, coins and books. The two men were friends and Townshend had owned property in the Fens, visiting Wisbech Museum on several occasions. Townshend's 6000 books were an important addition to the Museum Library, originally founded by the Wisbech Literary Society in 1781.
(Wisbech & Fenland Museum)

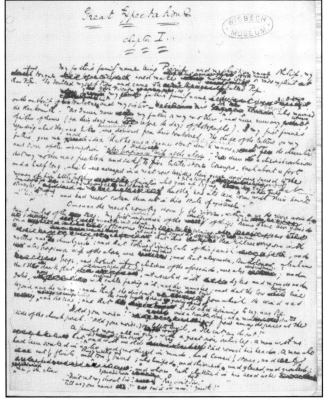

8: 1870-1879

WISBECH MAYORS	
1870	Robert Wherry
1871	Frederic Ford
1872	Frederic Ford
1873	Frederic Ford
1874	John Minnitt Mason
1875	Frederic Ford
1876	Charles Gane
1877	Charles Gane
1878	John William Stanley
1879	John William Stanley

← ———————— VIII. Wisbech as depicted on Sheet 65 of the 1st edition one-inch Ordnance Survey map. Originally published on 1st March 1824, this revised engraving printed in 1870 included the two railway stations. Using the alternative spelling WISBEACH the map also names the Gas Works and Cemetery in Leverington Road, and the Eight-Sail Mill and Union House along Lynn Road. This map is reproduced at 1in to 1 mile. (A.Ingram collection)

72. All Saints Church, Walsoken where the funeral service for Richard Young took place on Saturday 21st October 1871. He had died suddenly in London on 15th October aged 62; just two days after being elected Sheriff of London and Middlesex. Wisbech was notified by telegram and his body returned to the town by train the following Friday. All Wisbech shops and businesses closed between 10am and 12 noon as a mark of respect. He was buried in Walsoken churchyard, with a stained glass chancel window being dedicated to his memory in 1873 by Mrs Young and her eight children. (Wisbech & Fenland Museum)

73.   This memorial in the Octagon Church graveyard is to Sarah Bell, who died on 7th July 1871 aged 30 years. When the Octagon opened in January 1831 it was only licensed for burials. The first funeral service took place four months later on 13th May when Henry John Holmes of Wisbech, aged 11 months, was laid to rest in the graveyard. In 1832 a 21ft burial plot cost £1 1s 0d whilst a 42ft plot including brickwork cost £2 12s 6d. Rev T.P.Holmes died in office aged 83 after being incumbent of the Octagon Church for 47 years. He was buried in this graveyard on Thursday 22nd February 1877. (A.Ingram/ Wisbech Parish Church)

74.   Wisbech Prison was built in 1846 to re-place the House of Correction in Gaol Lane. Costing about £13,000 to build, its design was based on Pentonville Gaol in London. The Isle magistrates met here to hold their courts until October 1855 when they moved to the Sessions House. With crime in Wisbech decreasing this prison in Victoria Road closed on 15th May 1878. The Governor Mr Burrows retired whilst the re-maining inmates held in its 43 cells were trans-ferred to Cambridge Gaol.
(Lilian Ream Exhibition Gallery)

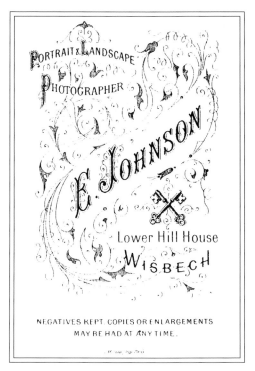

75.   Sophia Doughty, this 13-year-old brown-eyed girl, was convicted on 13th October 1873 of stealing a pair of women's drawers. She was sentenced to 21 days imprisonment in Wisbech Prison followed by five years at Bristol Reformatory. The Wisbech Prison Particular Descriptions ledger for 1870-1872 contained photographs and personal details on three hundred prisoners. Following closure the prison building was sold to Henry Farrow and then demolished, the Governor's house being converted into a private residence. (Wisbech & Fenland Museum)

76.   The opening ceremony for the North Cambridgeshire Hospital on Thursday 2nd October 1873, photographed by Edward Johnson. Miss Trafford-Southwell, the founder and benefactor, was a descendant of an old Wisbech family. She laid the foundation stone of this 26-bed cottage hospital and paid for its construction, furnishings and surgical instruments. The first patient was admitted on 22nd November, but initially there was no outpatient department or dispensary. She continued to support the hospital with generous donations until her death in November 1879. (Wisbech & Fenland Museum)

77.   On 10th January 1837 the 'Guardians of the Poor of the Wisbech Union' purchased land adjoining the Eight-Sail mill to build the Union Workhouse. Designed in the Elizabethan style and opened in March 1838 it could accommodate about 600 inmates from 22 parishes. Rev Fardell, Vicar of St Peter's Church became the first chairman of the Board of Guardians, a post he held until his death in March 1854. Kelly's Directory for 1875 stated that the *Workhouse is capable of containing 475 inmates, and averages 200 inmates.* (G.Drew collection)

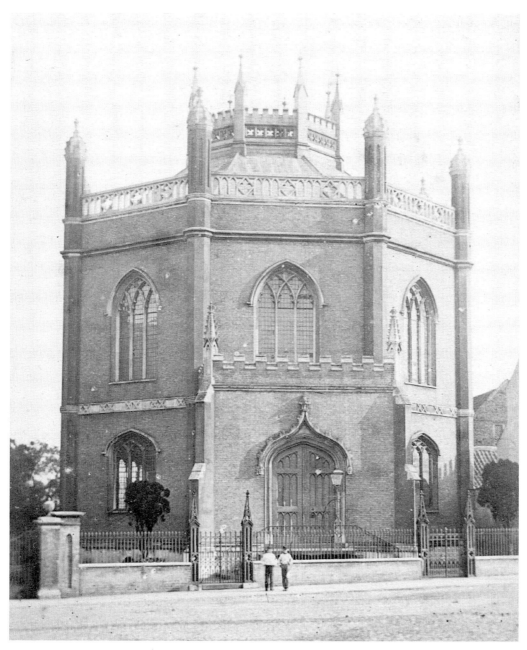

78.   Rev Charles Cecil Sumner, former curate at Walpole St Peter, began his ministry at the Octagon on Saturday 21st July 1877. During his incumbency the galleries and pulpit were moved, and the choir brought down from the galleries into the chancel. The first Octagon baptism took place on 11th February 1878 when Henry and Catherine Silburn presented their daughter Edith Mary. Rev Sumner seems to have been a man of great energy and determination, but with a great bent for sarcasm which caused some ill feeling. In the mid-1880s congregations began to dwindle and he felt that a new incumbent would be better for the well being of the church. (G.Drew collection)

79.   A typical Victorian portrait of mother and child by Enoch Steele, listed as a photographer in Kelly's Directories from 1869-1875. This is a carte-de-visite - a photograph stuck on to a backing card bearing the photographer's name and address - which were produced between 1854 and 1890. Special albums were manufactured to hold these family photographs and commercially produced portraits of the famous and infamous. In July 1860 Queen Victoria had portraits taken of herself, Prince Albert and their children which sold in millions.
(A.Ingram collection)

A comprehensive history of the Wisbech Canal can be found in the companion album *Branch Line to Upwell.*

80.   Algernon Peckover, the youngest son of Jonathan and Susannah Peckover, was born on 25th November 1803. Following his marriage in 1828 to Priscilla, a banker's daughter, they moved into Sibald's Holme along North Brink. Algernon and his eldest brother William became bankers in the business founded by their father Jonathan, and were instrumental in founding Wisbech Museum. Algernon served the town as a Councillor from 1839 to 1847 and an Alderman from 1847 to 1859. Following his brother William's death in 1877 Algernon was appointed Borough Treasurer. (Wisbech & Fenland Museum)

81.   Mrs Mayer's Asylum built in 1815 beside the Wisbech Canal, in a painting by Algernon Peckover. As a gifted amateur architect Algernon designed Wisteria House and Harecroft House [1844] and the new Friends Meeting House [1854] along North Brink. He also gave generously towards the Wisbech Museum's Reading Room where each week he would meet Samuel Smith to sort and display artefacts, including the photographs and coins they had donated. Algernon Peckover died on 10th December 1893 leaving a personal fortune of over £1 million, and was laid to rest in The Friends burial-ground. (Margaret Cave collection)

82.   The banking hall adjoining Bank House eventually became inadequate and this new building on the right was erected in the Old Market. Designed by E.Boardman and with strongrooms fitted with Hobbs' fire and burglar-proof doors, Gurney's Bank opened to the public on Wednesday 23rd April 1879. Following Alexander Peckover's retirement from the firm in 1893 it became known as the Gurney, Birkbeck, Barclay and Buxton Bank. On 10th June 1896 this, and a number of other private banks, were amalgamated into Barclay and Co Ltd. (Wisbech & Fenland Museum)

9: 1880-1889

IX.   The Old Horse Fair (centre) on this 1st edition 25in to 1 mile OS map published in 1885. For over 200 years a horse fair was held here on the Wednesday prior to Whit Sunday. In 1810 it was moved to the cattle market in Chapel Road. By 1881 the population of Wisbech stood at 9249, this was 68 less than in 1871 and represented a 9% decrease from the 1851 figure of 10,178. (Fenland coll.)

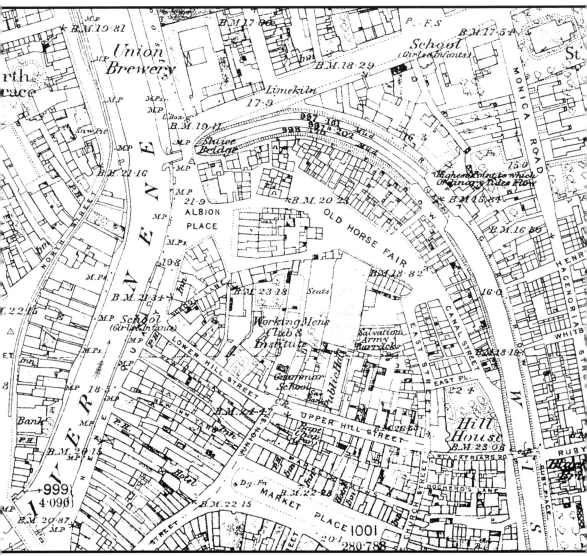

83.   Marshall George Strapps, seen here sitting in the midday sun by his Toll Gate in Leverington Road. The powers of the Wisbech and Thorney Turnpike Trust had expired on 1st November 1880, thus allowing vehicles and livestock to pass without payment. Toll Gates also stood at the entrance to Wisbech along Lynn Road, Walsoken Road, Pickard's Lane, Elm Road and South Brink. In 1898 an early motorist described the road surface between Wisbech and Guyhirn as consisting of loose broken flints. Mr Strapps, who had been a postman and Librarian of the Wisbech Institute, was also an award-winning woodcarver and a collector of coins and curios.
(Wisbech & Fenland Museum)

84.   Mayor W.M.Rust had proposed the Mayoral Chain of Office for Wisbech during his 1882/83 term in office. Each link carried the name of a Mayor of Wisbech since 1835, with past mayors having contributed a link as a memorial of their year in office. A badge, donated by Algernon Peckover, depicted the common seal of the borough with the inscription *Insigne Municipale Wisbechiense*. The chain, all in 15 carat hallmarked gold, was first worn on 9th November 1883 when Mr Rust was elected for a second term. Mrs Young, widow of Richard Young MP, presented these mayoral scarlet robes of office.
(Wisbech & Fenland Museum)

GREAT EASTERN RAILWAY.

WISBECH & OUTWELL TRAMWAY.

OCTOBER, 1883.

TRAMCARS WILL RUN AS UNDER:—

WEEK DAYS.

	a.m.	a.m.	a.m.	p.m.	p.m.	p.m.
WISBECH STATION	7 10	9 30	11 40	2 40	4 45	6 45
ELM BRIDGE	7 28	9 50	12 0	2 58	5 5	7 3
BOYCE'S BRIDGE	7 42	10 5	12 15	3 12	5 20	7 17
OUTWELL BASIN	7 50	10 15	12 25	3 20	5 30	7 25

	a.m.	a.m.	p.m.	p.m.	p.m.	p.m.
OUTWELL BASIN	8 0	10 40	1 35	3 40	5 50	7 45
BOYCE'S BRIDGE	8 8	10 48	1 45	3 50	5 58	7 53
ELM BRIDGE	8 22	11 2	2 0	4 5	6 12	8 7
WISBECH STATION	8 40	11 20	2 20	4 25	6 30	8 25

The Tram Cars will stop for the purpose of setting down or taking up Passengers at any point along the line of route.

FARES ANY DISTANCE:—

First Class.

Third Class.

Personal Luggage not exceeding 28 lbs. in weight will be allowed to be taken by each Adult Passenger free of charge if carried by hand.

MERCHANDISE TRAFFIC
Will be dealt with at the following Sidings or Depots:—

ELM BRIDGE, BOYCE'S BRIDGE, OUTWELL BASIN.

Very moderate charges for haulage will be made, particulars of these and other information can be obtained from the Company's Inspectors at the Depots, from the Station Agent at Wisbech, the District Goods Manager at Cambridge, or the Goods Manager at Liverpool Street.

WILLIAM BIRT, General Manager.

5902   Printed at the Company's Works, Stratford.

85.   James West Stanton, a teacher at the Barton School, was appointed Churchwarden at the Octagon in 1884. Together with his elder brother they had been associated with the management of Barton School, founded by their father. Following the appointment of his elder brother Rev W.R.Stanton as headmaster of Wisbech Grammar School, James became headmaster of Barton School.
(Wisbech & Fenland Museum)

86.   Clarkson Mill, a picturesque four-sail wooden postmill, was purchased by Norwich brewers Steward & Patteson in May 1886 and then demolished. Built about 1690 and owned by Messrs Anderson in the early 1800s, William Clarke was at the mill in 1863 and 1873. Prior to 1877 the adjacent Clarkson Inn public house had been named the Windmill Inn. Marshall George Strapps made a fine model of Clarkson Mill from one of its oak timbers and donated it to Wisbech Museum. The mill had stood on a mound opposite the Lynn Road/ Clarkson Avenue junction. (Wisbech & Fenland Museum)

87.   An Edward Johnson photograph taken from the Canal Sluice looking along Lynn Road towards The Park. To the left of the mill stands an early 19th century building with window shutters that was raised to three storeys circa 1860. By 1883 local photographer Valentine Blanchard had founded his studio in Lynn Road, later taken over by John Hinley and then Alfred Drysdale. Abraham Plumb the timber, slate and coal merchant whose premises are on the right, appeared in Kelly's Directories from 1875 to 1888. (Lilian Ream Exhibition Gallery)

88.   Bowles Mill, situated in Magazine Lane close to Elgoods Brewery, was purchased by William Bowles for £850 on 14th May 1887. Built around 1772 this tower mill had previously been worked by his father Stephen who sold flour at the family shop in the Old Market. The Third Cambridgeshire Regiment of Volunteer Infantry was formed in 1808 and commanded by Colonel Watson to defend Wisbech against attack from Napoleon Bonaparte.   Their ammunition was stored near the mill, hence the name Magazine Lane. (Lilian Ream Exhibition Gallery)

89.   A group of Wisbech cyclists pose with their machines circa 1887. On the left is a 46in front wheel Penny Farthing or 'Ordinary' bicycle, with a larger 52in model on the right. The girl is riding a 34in child's 'Cheylesmore' tricycle whilst the couple own a 'Sociable' tricycle costing £30. The young man spent £17 on his Singer Extra-Ordinary with treadle-action pedals and is wearing narrow leg trousers to avoid catching his clothing in the solid-tyre wheels. At a Town Council meeting on Friday 6th September 1898 Councillor Collins said *seven miles an hour through the principal streets was quite fast enough for bicycles, which went so quickly and softly.* (P.Foster collection)

19mm

90.   Gold and silver coins were redesigned for Queen Victoria's Golden Jubilee in 1887. The original silver sixpence design (right) closely resembled a half-sovereign, which prompted unscrupulous individuals to gild them and deceive the public. They were therefore withdrawn after a few months and replaced with a 'wreath of oak & olive leaves' design (above) first introduced by William IV, which had also featured on early Victorian sixpences. (C.Cooke)

91.   A Golden Jubilee Celebration Dinner in the Market Place at 1pm on Tuesday 21st June 1887. Two thousand employees sat down to enjoy a meal of cold joints of meat and hot plum puddings, served up by their friends and employers. Earlier in the day a large procession, starting from the Town Hall, had stopped at the junction of Chapel Road and Pickard's Lane. There Mrs Dawbarn the Mayoress planted a Wellingtonia tree which became known as the Jubilee tree. Queen Victoria celebrated three Jubilees, but there were no official celebrations for her Silver Jubilee in 1862 that fell just six months after the death of her beloved Prince Albert. (Lilian Ream Exhibition Gallery)

92.   In 1888 Rev Sumner moved to Suffolk, becoming the Rector of St Andrew's, Melton. He had exchanged churches with Rev Charles Sumpter Harris who became the new incumbent of the Octagon Church on Sunday 7th October 1888. Educated at Trinity Hall, Cambridge, he was an inspiring evangelical preacher, and his son played the organ. Following his death in 1894 a resolution in the minutes book of the trustees recorded their gratitude to him for 'his spiritual ministration'. They also remarked on the wonderful way in which he had carried on in spite of his disability - he was totally blind! (Wisbech & Fenland Museum)

93.   The double-florin, a new coin design introduced in Jubilee year to compliment the florin, was abandoned after only four years. This four-shilling piece was easily confused with the five-shilling crown as larger Jubilee silver coin designs did not include an indication of value. By tradition a new monarch's portrait on the obverse [heads] side of a coin always faced in the opposite direction to its predecessor. (C.Cooke)

36mm

10: 1890-1899

94. Built in the late 18th century to replace an earlier wooden post-mill, this eight-sail tower mill was owned by the Bishop of Ely in 1800 and let to John Goward of Chatteris. The Mill was sold by auction to James Pollard in 1871, Thomas Godfrey in 1887, and to Frank Leach for £1120 on 6th February 1891. One sail that fell off in 1863 was soon replaced, but after two sails were blown into The Park on 24th March 1895 the remaining six were dismantled in 1897. (Lilian Ream Exhibition Gallery)

WISBECH MAYORS

1890	Henry Farrow
1891	Henry Farrow
1892	George Carrick
1893	Alfred William May
1894	Alfred William May
1895	Robinson Smith
1896	Edwin Bidwell Bellars
1897	Henry Farrow
1898	John Henry Foster
1899	William Shepherd Collins

95.   Skating match in progress at Horseshoe Corner, just across the road from Samuel Smith's home. Spectators line the half-mile long course, a snow ridge and flags dividing the lanes, with the name S.Loveday of Welney being chalked up on a board beside the starting barrel. In 1891 veteran fen skaters 'Turkey' Smart (61) and George 'Gutta Percha' See (59) strapped on their skates, known as 'pattens', for a friendly match. Thirty-six years earlier they had raced each other over this same course with 'Turkey' Smart becoming Champion Skater of the Fens. (P.Foster collection)

96.   At 9.50am Hardingham Mehew photographed this three-masted barque moored alongside Mill's Brewery on Nene Parade. In 1872 the Lynn brig *Arab*, an ex-slave trader, had capsized here and sank with her masts across the river. The Working Mens Institute clock tower had been erected through the generosity of the Peckover family and opened on 1st February 1892. The clock had formerly been housed in the gable end of the Lecture Hall behind. In the shadow of the tower stands the Welcome Coffee Tavern, managed by Mrs Rebecca Miller since 1888. (P.Foster collection)

97.   Originally the home of Mr Jecks, Barton School had been founded by William Redin Stanton circa 1850. A schoolroom, dormitories and heated swimming pool were added to create this private boarding school for about 100 boys. In the 19th century about 800 'Old Bartonians' received prizes and certificates at Oxford University. Each Sunday a long 'crocodile' of Bartonian boys walked 3/4 mile along Barton Lane, North Brink and Pickard's Lane to attend the Octagon Church. (A.Ingram collection)

98.   The earliest interior view of the Octagon Church, looking towards the chancel, altar and 'east' window - which actually faced north! Silver Communion Plate, consisting of two communion cups, three patens and a flagon had been donated to the Octagon by Dr. Jobson in 1829. Local silversmith George Lefever presented an altar piece in 1847, described as an ancient metal chasing of the Ascension. Boys from the Barton School, dressed in their Eton suits and wearing mortarboards, would fill pews on the left side of the nave every Sunday. (Wisbech & Fenland Museum)

Wisbech.

Barton S

99.   Lilian, the youngest daughter of Louisa and Thomas Pratt, was born at Ingleborough near Wisbech on Saturday 30th June 1877. Educated at Miss Bradley's private school in Wisbech Castle, she recalled being taken as a young girl to the Octagon Church by her eldest sister Louie. They had to arrive early before the Bartonians in order to secure a pew. In 1894 Lilian Pratt started work as a photographic apprentice with Alfred Drysdale at his Lynn Road studio, staying with the firm when it was taken over by Hardingham Mehew and Leonard Smith. (Lilian Ream Exhibition Gallery)

100.   Samuel Smith the amateur photographer was also an accomplished astronomer, entomologist, geologist, mechanic, mineralogist and palaeontologist. In addition he collected coins, tokens, shells and curios - earning him the affectionate nickname Mr 'Philosopher' Smith. He passed away on Monday 18th July 1892 aged 90, with the funeral service taking place in Leverington Road Cemetery chapel the following Friday. (Wisbech & Fenland Museum)

101.   Organised football had been played in Wisbech since the 1880s. Wisbech Town Club, who had changed their name from Wisbech St Augustine's on 19th August 1892, played at the Flint House ground in Lynn Road. Goal nets were used for the first time in Wisbech at this ground on 26th December 1892 when Wisbech played Grantham. The 1893/94 season kicked off on 19th September with a floodlit local derby match against Lynn Town at The Walks. Under primitive electric lighting, and with a white-painted ball that soon turned muddy-brown, Wisbech Town managed to win 5-1.
(Lilian Ream Exhibition Gallery)

38mm

102.   On the edge of each 'old head' crown in Roman numerals was the regnal year - reckoned from the anniversary of Victoria's accession in 1837. Therefore these 1893 crowns either bore the year LVI [56th] or the scarcer LVII [57th]. The reverse design featured St George & Dragon, which also appeared on the gold coinage. Between 1893 and 1900 the Royal Mint produced 2,161,136 silver crowns, the last period large quantities were issued for general circulation. (C.Cooke)

103.   Rev Robert Buckley Boyer was appointed to the Octagon Church in 1894 and commenced his duties on Sunday 29th July. He had previously been Superintendent of the Mission to Seamen for over 30 years. Sadly he died after only six months in office on 12th January 1895 and was succeeded at the Octagon by his son Rev Richard Boyer. A market had been held here since Saxon times for by 1221 this area was already called the Old Market. (Wisbech & Fenland Museum)

104. Wisbech-born Octavia Hill, inspired by her parents ideals, worked to improve living conditions of the poor in London through 'friendly housing management'. In an area of Marylebone known as 'Little Hell' she set out to train *a rough population into habits of order, cleanliness and self-respect* with a sensitive, caring and humane approach. She also battled against development in order to retain open spaces for people to enjoy. Her campaign with Canon Hardwick Rawnsley and solicitor Sir Robert Hunter *to preserve places of historic interest or natural beauty for ever, for everyone* led to The National Trust's formation in 1895. (Octavia Hill Birthplace Museum Trust)

105. Tea on the Market Place for 2500 children on Tuesday 22nd June 1897 - a day of festivities to mark Queen Victoria's Diamond Jubilee. In the morning a procession, led by the town's combined Sunday Schools, had paraded through packed streets to St Peter's Church. Rev Boyer of the Octagon took part in this service of thanksgiving, the sermon being preached by Rev Crossley, vicar of St Augustine's. Earlier in the day whilst 2000 employees were enjoying a Dinner on the Market Place the Mayor Councillor Bellars received a telegram from Her Majesty which read: *From my heart I thank my beloved people. May God bless them. The sun is shining brightly. V.R. and I.* (Wisbech & Fenland Museum)

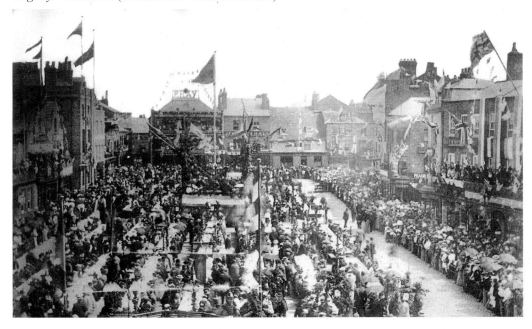

106.   In 1897 this drinking fountain, designed by Mr Armstead, was erected in the Old Market opposite the Octagon Church. Dedicated to the memory of Mr & Mrs George Duppa Collins of Wisbech by their daughters, Mrs Pocock and Mrs Prankard, it was presented to the Corporation on Thursday 17th June. Mr Collins practised as a solicitor and served as Clerk to the Wisbech Board of Guardians from 1837 to 1875. The inscription read *Honest Water, which ne'er left man I' the mire.* (Wisbech & Fenland Museum)

107.   The Collins fountain and Octagon Church, photographed in November 1898. Rev Richard Boyer commenced his ministry at the Octagon on 19th April 1895, holding services at 11am and 7pm each Sunday. Educated at Gonville and Caius College, Cambridge he was ordained in 1887 and upon their arrival in Wisbech Rev and Mrs Boyer lived at 10 North Brink. In the 18th century Jane Stuart, the illegitimate daughter of King James II, lived in Wisbech. Whilst her half-sister Mary became Queen of England, Jane is reputed to have lived and spun thread in the basement of the whitewashed building seen here next to the Octagon. (Cambridgeshire Collection)

108.   Frederic John Gardiner wrote a *History of Wisbech and Neighbourhood 1848-1898,* the last of several town histories published during the 19th century. Son of John Gardiner, founder of the Wisbech Advertiser, his book was produced at their printing works in 1898. The List of Subscribers included many notable Wisbech families. Queen Victoria requested that a copy be forwarded to Windsor, whilst the Prince and Princess of Wales asked if a copy might be sent to Sandringham House.
(Wisbech & Fenland Museum)

109.   The Grammar School moved from St Peter's Church into these Upper Hill Street premises in 1549. Following the Reformation and dissolution of church-endowed schools, King Edward VI had granted Wisbech Grammar School a charter *for the instruction of boys and young men in grammatical knowledge and polite learning.* The Capital Burgesses also held their meetings in this building from 1549 until 1810. This photograph was taken shortly before pupils moved to a new building on South Brink. (Wisbech & Fenland Museum)

110.   School Room of the new Wisbech Grammar School, opened by the Mayor Alderman Farrow on 20th January 1898. Boys would assemble in this finely panelled room for Morning Prayer, after which it was used by the Junior Department for teaching purposes. Formerly the home of George Duppa Collins, the foundation stone for these adapted and extended school premises had been laid by Alexander Peckover, the Lord Lieutenant of Cambridgeshire. The Peckover family had subscribed a total of £3615 towards the new school buildings. The Headmaster Arthur Poyser had also held this post at the old premises since 1890. (D.Chesters collection)

X.   This Wisbech Grammar School badge was based on the common seal adopted by the Corporation of Wisbech in 1549. It depicts full-length figures of St Peter and St Paul, patrons of the parish church, beneath canopies in the Renaissance style. Wisbech Grammar School Old Boys have included anti-slavery campaigner Thomas Clarkson and Thomas Herring, Archbishop of Canterbury from 1747-1751. (Wisbech Grammar School)

111.   A steam fire pump outside Saunders, the circus tent & cloth manufacturers along Nene Quay. The new Borough Fire Station in Lower Hill Street, opened in 1898, replaced the Pump Room within Wisbech Castle Grounds where two manually operated pumps had been housed since June 1855. With horses stabled behind the Rose & Crown and station key at the Police Office adjoining the Cattle Market, getting the Brigade moving had been time-consuming. The first Shand & Mason steam fire engine for Wisbech cost £800 and was named *The Etty* by Mayoress Mrs Peatling on 18th March 1895. (Lilian Ream Exhibition Gallery)

MANTLES, ULSTERS, WATERPROOFS,
SHAWLS
CARPETS
* SALE *
ANNUAL
STOCK-TAKING
BARGAINS
IN
Furs, Rugs, Blankets,
REMNANTS of ALL SORTS.
AT CHAS. B. ANDERSON'S
WISBECH.
IS NOW
PLACE.
DRESSES
CURTAINS
Cheap Lots of HOSIERY & GLOVES,
RIBBONS, FRILLINGS,
LACE.
TAKING
ALL GOODS REDUCED DURING SALE.

112.   The Balding + Mansell composing room staff at Park Works, where on 1st August 1892 the printing partnership between Mr Balding and Mr Mansell was established. Alfred Balding had opened his own printing works at 11 Nene Quay in 1869. Ernest Mansell, who had served a seven-year apprenticeship as a lithographer, answered his advertisement for a partner. Alfred Balding left the partnership two years later, but the business name of Balding + Mansell was retained. (J.Hill collection)

113.　Bridge Street, photographed from the National Provincial Bank, with the Iron Bridge in the foreground. In the centre is a memorial to Thomas Clarkson, unveiled on 11th November 1881 by the Rt Hon Bouverie Brand MP, Speaker of the House of Commons. To its right stands the Post Office, opened on 1st February 1887 and built on the site of Richard Young's offices. Between the Post Office and the Eagle Tavern we can see J.T.Jeffery's hardware store and Charles Exley the wine & spirit merchant, who were both trading in Bridge Street between 1892 and 1900. (C.Regester/A.Ingram)

WISBECH STREET NAMES

19th Century	21st Century	19th Century	21st Century
Agenoria Street	St Augustine's Road	Norfolk Street West	West Street
Cemetery Road	Kings Walk	North Terrace	North End
Canal Row	Falcon Road	Paradise Walk	Bowthorpe Road
George Street	Elizabeth Terrace	Pickards Lane	Harecroft Rd/Chapel Rd
Goal Lane	Queens Rd/Somers Rd	Quere Street	King Street
Great Church Street	Alexandra Road	Rameth Road	Ramnoth Road
Great South Street	John Thompson Road	Sheep Market	Exchange Square
Horseshoe Lane	Peatlings Lane	South End	Elm Road
Jumps Walk	Elizabeth Terrace	Stafford Place	Wellington Terrace
Little South Street	West Street	Timber Market	Norfolk Street
Marsh Walk	Park Road	Union Row	West Street
Marshland Street	Norwich Street	Walsoken Road	Norwich Road
Monica Road	St Augustine's Road	Water Lane	Royal Place
Nelson Street	John F Kennedy Court	Wheatsheaf Place	Royal Place

114.   An interior view of the Angel public house in Great Church Street. By 1898 there were 79 licensed establishments in Wisbech, including 49 fully licensed houses and 21 beer houses. In the early 19th century there were no restrictions on pub opening times, but in 1854 campaigners, led by the Temperance Movement, forced them to close at midnight on Saturdays. Apart from Sunday lunch and evening they remained closed until 4pm on Monday. From 1864 pubs had to close every night from 1am to 4am, then in August 1872 the Licensing Act further restricted the sale of intoxicating liquors. (Lilian Ream Exhibition Gallery)

ARSENIC IN BEER.

ELM ROAD BREWERY,
WISBECH.

SAMPLES of these well-known Ales have been taken and submitted to the PUBLIC ANALYST Who Certifies them to be

ABSOLUTELY FREE FROM ARSENIC OR ANY OTHER DELETERIOUS SUBSTANCE.

This UNBIASSED REPORT shows that Consumers may have every Confidence in

F. WOODS' HOME-BREWED ALES.

BUY ALES that are guaranteed to be absolutely Pure and Wholesome and free from any injurious substance.

REGISTRY OFFICE FOR SERVANTS.

Servants Requiring Situations
SHOULD APPLY EARLY TO

S. & M. FALKNER,

DRAPERS, &c., REGENT HOUSE, WISBECH.

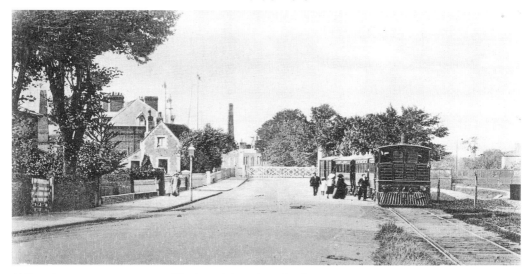

115.   A steam tram pauses at Elm Road Crossing, the first stop along a six-mile route to Upwell. Passengers would board the tramcars where tickets for their journey were issued by a conductor-guard, seen here walking from his luggage van. In the background are gates for the main line to King's Lynn, which crossed Wisbech Canal on the right. By the lamppost is the crossing keeper's cottage, whilst on the horizon stands the chimney of Brewin's steam-powered corn mill. (A.Ingram collection)

116.   The National Provincial banking hall in Wisbech circa 1900. A Wisbech Trustee Savings Bank had been established in 1818 to encourage thrift amongst the poor. Open every Friday and Saturday the bank was originally based in the Jury Room of the Sessions House. Trading was transferred to the Butter Cross until about 1847 when the business moved into bank premises in Upper Hill Street. Most account holders withdrew their funds following the establishment of a Post Office Savings Bank in 1861. (NatWest)

117.   The name farthing originates from the Old English 'feorthing' meaning 'a fourth part'. Round silver farthing coins were introduced in England by Edward I in 1279. Our Anglo-Saxon ancestors had obtained small change by cutting silver pennies into halves or quarters. The 'old' or 'veiled

head' was introduced on Victorian gold and silver coinage in 1893 and on bronze coins from 1895. From 1897 until 1918 bronze farthings were minted with a dark finish to avoid confusion with sovereigns. By 1901 farthings were the smallest denomination coin minted for use in Britain. (C.Cooke)

20mm

118. Children gathered around a Christmas Tree in Nelson Street, Wisbech circa 1901. This tradition became popular in Britain after Prince Albert brought a tree to Windsor Castle in 1841 for the Royal Family. Originally they were decorated with apples, cakes and sweets, but Christmas tree angels and glass ornaments were imported from Germany in the 1870s. By 1890 candles were being replaced by mass-produced Christmas tree lights and within ten years department stores had introduced large illuminated trees to lure customers.
(C.Regester/A.Ingram)

WISBECH MAYORS	
1900	William Shepherd Collins
1901	John Goward

A comprehensive history of the Wisbech & Upwell Tramway can be found in the companion album *Branch Line to Upwell.*

119. Queen Victoria passed away on Tuesday 22nd January 1901 at the age of 81. This illustration appeared in the *Wisbech Advertiser* and *Wisbech Standard*, with both newspapers inserting mourning borders into an otherwise normal front-page layout filled with advertisements. Victoria died at Osborne House on the Isle of Wight having reigned longer than any previous monarch. On a bright and beautiful Saturday 2nd February 1901 all the business establishments and offices in Wisbech remained closed. At 11am the Town Band played a Dead March on the Market Place before proceeding to the Octagon Church for a memorial service, led by Rev R.Boyer. (Fenland coll.)

120. The album finishes as it started with a view of St Peter's Church. A muffled peal from the bells in St Peter's Church tower echoed over Wisbech as the civic procession, led by the Volunteer Band's muffled drums, left the Corn Exchange. Representatives from all walks of life marched slowly through streets packed with thousands of mourners towards St Peter's. In his address the Rev J.Thomas said the Queen *had won the enthusiastic love of her people and the veneration of the whole world.* (Lilian Ream Exhibition Gallery)

MP Middleton Press

Easebourne Lane, Midhurst, W Sussex. GU29 9AZ Tel: 01730 813169 Fax: 01730 812601
*If books are not available from your local transport stockist, order direct with cheque,
Visa or Mastercard, post free UK.*

BRANCH LINES

Branch Line to Allhallows
Branch Line to Alton
Branch Lines around Ascot
Branch Line to Ashburton
Branch Lines around Bodmin
Branch Line to Bude
Branch Lines around Canterbury
Branch Lines around Chard & Yeovil
Branch Line to Cheddar
Branch Lines around Cromer
Branch Lines to East Grinstead
Branch Lines of East London
Branch Lines to Effingham Junction
Branch Lines around Exmouth
Branch Lines to Falmouth, Helston & St. Ives
Branch Line to Fairford
Branch Lines around Gosport
Branch Line to Hayling
Branch Lines to Henley, Windsor & Marlow
Branch Line to Hawkhurst
Branch Lines around Huntingdon
Branch Line to Ilfracombe
Branch Line to Kingswear
Branch Line to Lambourn
Branch Lines to Launceston & Princetown
Branch Line to Looe
Branch Line to Lyme Regis
Branch Lines around Midhurst
Branch Line to Minehead
Branch Line to Moretonhampstead
Branch Lines to Newport
Branch Lines to Newquay
Branch Lines around North Woolwich
Branch Line to Padstow
Branch Lines around Plymouth
Branch Lines to Seaton and Sidmouth
Branch Lines around Sheerness
Branch Line to Shrewsbury
Branch Line to Swanage *updated*
Branch Line to Tenterden
Branch Lines around Tiverton
Branch Lines to Torrington
Branch Line to Upwell
Branch Lines of West London
Branch Lines around Weymouth
Branch Lines around Wimborne
Branch Lines around Wisbech

NARROW GAUGE

Branch Line to Lynton
Branch Lines around Portmadoc 1923-46
Branch Lines around Porthmadog 1954-94
Branch Line to Southwold
Douglas to Port Erin
Douglas to Peel
Kent Narrow Gauge
Northern France Narrow Gauge
Romneyrail
Southern France Narrow Gauge
Sussex Narrow Gauge
Two-Foot Gauge Survivors
Vivarais Narrow Gauge

SOUTH COAST RAILWAYS

Ashford to Dover
Bournemouth to Weymouth
Brighton to Worthing
Eastbourne to Hastings
Hastings to Ashford
Portsmouth to Southampton
Ryde to Ventnor
Southampton to Bournemouth

SOUTHERN MAIN LINES

Basingstoke to Salisbury
Bromley South to Rochester
Crawley to Littlehampton
Dartford to Sittingbourne
East Croydon to Three Bridges
Epsom to Horsham
Exeter to Barnstaple
Exeter to Tavistock
Faversham to Dover
London Bridge to East Croydon
Orpington to Tonbridge
Tonbridge to Hastings
Salisbury to Yeovil
Sittingbourne to Ramsgate
Swanley to Ashford
Tavistock to Plymouth
Three Bridges to Brighton
Victoria to Bromley South
Victoria to East Croydon
Waterloo to Windsor
Waterloo to Woking
Woking to Portsmouth
Woking to Southampton
Yeovil to Exeter

EASTERN MAIN LINES

Barking to Southend
Ely to Kings Lynn
Ely to Norwich
Fenchurch Street to Barking
Ipswich to Saxmundham
Liverpool Street to Ilford
Saxmundham to Yarmouth
Tilbury Loop

WESTERN MAIN LINES

Didcot to Swindon
Ealing to Slough
Exeter to Newton Abbot
Newton Abbot to Plymouth
Newbury to Westbury
Paddington to Ealing
Paddington to Princes Risborough
Plymouth to St. Austell
Princes Risborough to Banbury
Reading to Didcot
Slough to Newbury
St. Austell to Penzance
Taunton to Exeter
Westbury to Taunton

MIDLAND MAIN LINES

Euston to Harrow & Wealdstone
St. Pancras to St. Albans

COUNTRY RAILWAY ROUTES

Abergavenny to Merthyr
Andover to Southampton
Bath to Evercreech Junction
Bournemouth to Evercreech Junction
Burnham to Evercreech Junction
Cheltenham to Andover
Croydon to East Grinstead
Didcot to Winchester
East Kent Light Railway
Fareham to Salisbury
Guildford to Redhill
Reading to Basingstoke
Reading to Guildford
Redhill to Ashford
Salisbury to Westbury
Stratford upon Avon to Cheltenham
Strood to Paddock Wood
Taunton to Barnstaple
Wenford Bridge to Fowey
Westbury to Bath
Woking to Alton
Yeovil to Dorchester

GREAT RAILWAY ERAS

Ashford from Steam to Eurostar
Clapham Junction 50 years of change
Festiniog in the Fifties
Festiniog in the Sixties
Festiniog 50 years of enterprise
Isle of Wight Lines 50 years of change
Railways to Victory 1944-46
Return to Blaenau 1970-82
SECR Centenary album
Talyllyn 50 years of change
Yeovil 50 years of change

LONDON SUBURBAN RAILWAYS

Caterham and Tattenham Corner
Charing Cross to Dartford
Clapham Jn. to Beckenham Jn.
Crystal Palace (HL) & Catford Loop
East London Line
Finsbury Park to Alexandra Palace
Holbourn Viaduct to Lewisham
Kingston and Hounslow Loops
Lewisham to Dartford
Lines around Wimbledon
London Bridge to Addiscombe
Mitcham Junction Lines
North London Line
South London Line
West Croydon to Epsom
West London Line
Willesden Junction to Richmond
Wimbledon to Beckenham
Wimbledon to Epsom

STEAMING THROUGH

Steaming through Cornwall
Steaming through the Isle of Wight
Steaming through Kent
Steaming through West Hants
Steaming through West Sussex

TRAMWAY CLASSICS

Aldgate & Stepney Tramways
Barnet & Finchley Tramways
Bath Tramways
Brighton's Tramways
Bristol's Tramways
Burton & Ashby Tramways
Camberwell & W.Norwood Tramways
Clapham & Streatham Tramways
Croydon's Tramways
Dover's Tramways
East Ham & West Ham Tramways
Edgware and Willesden Tramways
Eltham & Woolwich Tramways
Embankment & Waterloo Tramways
Enfield & Wood Green Tramways
Exeter & Taunton Tramways
Greenwich & Dartford Tramways
Hammersmith & Hounslow Tramways
Hampstead & Highgate Tramways
Hastings Tramways
Holborn & Finsbury Tramways
Ilford & Barking Tramways
Kingston & Wimbledon Tramways
Lewisham & Catford Tramways
Liverpool Tramways 1. Eastern Routes
Liverpool Tramways 2. Southern Routes
Liverpool Tramways 3. Northern Routes
Maidstone & Chatham Tramways
Margate to Ramsgate
North Kent Tramways
Norwich Tramways
Reading Tramways
Seaton & Eastbourne Tramways
Shepherds Bush & Uxbridge Tramways
Southend-on-sea Tramways
Southwark & Deptford Tramways
Stamford Hill Tramways
Twickenham & Kingston Tramways
Victoria & Lambeth Tramways
Waltham Cross & Edmonton Tramways
Walthamstow & Leyton Tramways
Wandsworth & Battersea Tramways

TROLLEYBUS CLASSICS

Croydon Trolleybuses
Derby Trolleybuses
Hastings Trolleybuses
Huddersfield Trolleybuses
Maidstone Trolleybuses
Portsmouth Trolleybuses
Woolwich & Dartford Trolleybuses

WATERWAY ALBUMS

Kent and East Sussex Waterways
London to Portsmouth Waterway
West Sussex Waterways

MILITARY BOOKS

Battle over Portsmouth
Battle over Sussex 1940
Bombers over Sussex 1943-45
Bognor at War
Military Defence of West Sussex
Military Signals from the South Coast
Secret Sussex Resistance
Surrey Home Guard

OTHER RAILWAY BOOKS

Index to all Middleton Press stations
Industrial Railways of the South-East
South Eastern & Chatham Railways
London Chatham & Dover Railway
War on the Line (SR 1939-45)

BIOGRAPHY

Garraway Father & Son